Little Sweet Thing

Roy Williams

Methuen Drama

Published by Methuen 2005

1 3 5 7 9 10 8 6 4 2

First published in 2005 by
Methuen Publishing Limited
215 Vauxhall Bridge Road
London SW1V 1EJ

Copyright © 2005 by Roy Williams

Roy Williams has asserted his rights under the
Copyright, Designs and Patents Act, 1988,
to be identified as the author of this work

Methuen Publishing Limited Reg. No. 3543167

A CIP catalogue record for this book is available
from the British Library

ISBN 0 413 77502 X

Typeset by Country Setting, Kingsdown, Kent
Printed and bound in Great Britain by
Bookmarque Ltd, Croydon, Surrey

To the staunch poets and players,
my deepest thanks

R.W.

The New Wolsey Theatre Ipswich in association
with Nottingham Playhouse Theatre Company and
Birmingham Repertory Theatre Company present

LITTLE SWEET THING

by Roy Williams

First performance at The New Wolsey Theatre,
Ipswich on 4 February 2005.

THE NEW WOLSEY
THEATRE IPSWICH

Since opening in 2001, The New Wolsey Theatre's ambition has been to produce, co-produce and collaborate on productions that are accessible, high quality and diverse. With over 70,000 tickets sold per year, two-thirds of our mailing list is now made up of new attenders. In 2003, The New Wolsey Theatre won the Arts Council England/Eclipse Award in recognition of its success in developing culturally diverse audiences and programming.

As one of the founding partners of the Eclipse Theatre project, we are delighted to be working alongside Nottingham Playhouse and Birmingham Repertory Theatre to produce this new play, commissioned by Eclipse Theatre from one of Britain's leading contemporary playwrights. We are particularly pleased that this Roy Williams world première, the third Eclipse Theatre production and a play which addresses contemporary experience so directly, has originated at the New Wolsey Theatre, and is being seen for the first time, on tour in regional venues up and down the country.

Peter Rowe Artistic Director
Sarah Holmes Chief Executive

www.wolseytheatre.co.uk

Nottingham Playhouse
theatre company

Nottingham Playhouse has a commitment to commissioning new work and has staged four world premières on its main stage in the past year; indeed, over the past three years 40% of our main stage productions have been new works and in the current season the proportion is higher still. This new writing has coincided with a 35% increase in attendance and nine theatre award nominations in the last two years.

The Playhouse has toured its work to over fifty towns and cities in the UK and abroad. It played host to the Eclipse theatre initiative for its first two years, producing *Moon on a Rainbow Shawl* and the record-breaking *Mother Courage and Her Children*. Nottingham Playhouse is delighted to be co-producing the third Eclipse production **Little Sweet Thing** with the New Wolsey Theatre, Ipswich and Birmingham Repertory Theatre.

Giles Croft Artistic Director
Stephanie Sirr Chief Executive

www.nottinghamplayhouse.co.uk

THE REP
Birmingham Repertory Theatre

Birmingham Repertory Theatre is one of Britain's leading national producing theatre companies. Under the Artistic Direction of Jonathan Church, The REP is enjoying great success with a busy and exciting programme.

The commissioning and production of new work lies at the core of The REP's programme. In 1998 the company launched The Door, a venue dedicated to the production and presentation of new work. It has produced world premières from a new generation of British playwrights including Abi Morgan, Moira Buffini, Bryony Lavery, Gurpreet Kaur Bhatti, Sarah Woods, Roy Williams, Kaite O'Reilly and Jonathan Harvey. The REP itself received The Peggy Ramsay Award for New Writing last year enabling us to develop and commission more new plays for the future.

The REP's productions regularly transfer to London, tour nationally and internationally. Recent transfers and tours have included *The Witches, Through The Woods, Of Mice And Men, A Doll's House, The Crucible, Celestina, Hamlet, The Ugly Eagle, The Old Masters, The Snowman, The Gift, Behsharam (Shameless)* and *The Ramayana*.

The REP is delighted to be a co-producer in the Eclipse Theatre Initiative and looks forward to hosting the next Eclipse production.

Jonathan Church Artistic Director
Stuart Rogers Executive Director
Ben Payne Associate Director (Literary)

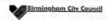

Welcome to the third production of Eclipse Theatre, this time being led by The New Wolsey Theatre, Ipswich. This follows last year's wonderfully successful national tour of *Mother Courage and Her Children* by Bertolt Brecht, adapted by Oladipo Agboluaje and set in contemporary war-torn West Africa, and the year before that the critically acclaimed production of *Moon On A Rainbow Shawl* by Errol John.

The Eclipse Theatre is an initiative supported by three producing theatres, Nottingham Playhouse, Birmingham Repertory Theatre and The New Wolsey Theatre. The initiative is funded by Arts Council England and was set up to develop the national profile of Black Middle Scale Regional Theatre.

In 2003 Eclipse Theatre also set up The Eclipse Theatre Writers' Lab, a project to develop ten up-and-coming Black Writers. In the autumn of 2004 it concluded, awarding five of the original ten writers a commission and individual placement at one of the following supporting theatres, to continue development of their work: West Yorkshire Playhouse, Contact Theatre Manchester, Birmingham Repertory Theatre, The New Wolsey Theatre, Ipswich and Nottingham Playhouse. The project was also supported by The National Theatre Studio and funded by Arts Council England, East Midlands, The Peggy Ramsay Foundation and Nottingham Playhouse.

When Eclipse Theatre began in 2002, I was proud to give our first ever writing commission to one of Britain's finest Black Writers. Roy Williams had just won The Evening Standard Award for *Clubland,* directed by Indu Rubasingham at The Royal Court Theatre, and everybody behind the Eclipse Theatre initiative was excited about him writing a play for regional theatre.

He came up with *Little Sweet Thing,* the show you are about to see. This fascinating, intriguing contemporary story was developed for Eclipse Theatre, with the help of Peter Rowe, Artistic Director of The New Wolsey Theatre, Michael Buffong, the Director, and a nod and a wink from me!

I truly hope you enjoy this show by Roy Williams.

Steven Luckie
Eclipse Theatre Producer

Following its run at The New Wolsey Theatre Ipswich (4th – 12th February 2005),
Little Sweet Thing tours to the following venues:

15-19 Feb	Nottingham Playhouse
22-26 Feb	Warwick Arts Centre
28 Feb – 5 Mar	Contact Theatre, Manchester
8-10 Mar	Northampton Theatres
16-19 Mar	Gardner Arts Centre, Brighton
29 Mar-2 Apr	West Yorkshire Playhouse
7-9 Apr	Birmingham Repertory Theatre
12–16 April	South Hill Park
19–23 April	Hampstead Theatre

(from left:) Roy Williams, Steven Luckie, Peter Rowe, Michael Buffong

CAST

In order of
appearance

Tash
Seroca Davis

Zoë
Lauren Taylor

Nathan
Ben Brooks

Miss Jules
Kay Bridgeman

Ryan
Glenn Hodge

Jamal
Richie Campbell

Kev
Marcel McCalla

Angela
Ashley Madekwe

'The Hood'

Director
Michael Buffong

Designer
Ruari Murchison

Choreographer
Kat

Fight Director
Renny Krupinski

Lighting Designer
Malcolm Rippeth

Sound Designer
Al Ashford

Voice Coach
Claudette Williams

Assistant Director
Steve Marmion

Casting Director
Sooki McShane

Production Manager
Dennis Charles

Technical Manager
Nikk Turnham

Company Stage Manager
Tracey J Cooper

Technical Stage Manager
Gary Wright

Deputy Stage Manager
Nina Scholar

Assistant Stage Manager
Michelle Dawkins

Technical ASM
Mark Richards

Costume Supervisor
Yvonne Milnes

Re-lights on tour
Matt Britten

Set constructed and painted by
Nottingham Playhouse

Stills photography
Mike Kwasniak

Production photography
Robert Day

Rehearsal photography
Ben King

THE COMPANY

KAY BRIDGEMAN
Miss Jules

Kay trained at Arden School of Theatre, Manchester. Television roles include Cassie Morigan in *Redcap* (BBC); Sharon in *The Eustace Brothers* (BBC, Dir. Paul Harrison); Valerie in *Doctors* (BBC); Lesley Bowe in *Holby City* (BBC); Aimie in *Murder in Mind* (BBC); Melissa in *Cutting It* (BBC); Karen Mays in *The Bill* (ITV) and Adelle in *Bhangra Heads* (HTV). Film includes Sandra in *Cherps*. Theatre includes Ildiko in *Car Thieves* (Fireraisers/Birmingham Rep); Yvonne in *Exclude Me* (Chelsea Theatre); Sharon in *Sing Yer Heart Out for the Lads* (Lyttleton Loft, Cottesloe); Olu, Bridie and Pepper in *Mules* (Contact Theatre); Cordelia in *King Lear* (Contact Theatre) and Leyla in *Talking in Tongues* (The Crucible Theatre). Kay played Yvonne in *Exclude Me* (BBC World Service Radio).

BEN BROOKS
Nathan

Ben is originally from Barmouth in North Wales and moved to London with his family at the age of eleven to pursue his love of acting. He trained at the Ravenscourt Theatre School and received a Diploma in Performing Arts at The London Studio Centre. He has many principal television credits to his name including Tom Baxter in *Aquila* (BBC), Thomas in *Captain Crimson* (BBC), Graham in *The Vice* and Samson in *Samson Superslug* (ITV). Recently he played Levi in *Talking Loud* by Trevor Williams at the Latchmere Theatre. Ben is very excited to be on his very first national tour.

RICHIE CAMPBELL
Jamal

Richie trained at Anna Scher Theatre School. He has appeared in *Cutter* (Half Moon Theatre/Lyric Hammersmith), *Slamdunk* (NITRO), *Aida* (Royal Opera House) and *This Island's Mine* (Millfield Theatre). Television and film includes *The Plague* (Prodigal Productions), *The Rulers, Dealers & Losers* (DDL Productions), *Just The Two of Us* (Leonardo Productions), *The Bill* (Thames TV), *Babyfather* (BBC) and *Have A Go Heroes* (BBC).

SEROCA DAVIS
Tash

Seroca trained at The Anna Scher Theatre, of which she has been a member since 1996. Film roles have included Teri in *Friends*, directed by Paul Whittington for Carlton/LFF; Leanne in *London Birds Can't Fly*, directed by Sarah Turner for Spirit Dance UK; Bully in *Kidscape - Anti-bullying*, directed by Ros Cook for Ragdoll Productions and Seroca in *Picture Power*, directed by Patrick Veale for Hawkshead. Television includes Beth Tyler in eight episodes of *The Bill* (Pearson); Jade in *Stuff of Life* (Tiger Aspect); Bianca Moor in *Holby City* (BBC); Jo in *London Transport Museum* (CLI); Yemi in *Coming Atcha* (two series – ITV); Melissa in *Homework High* (Channel 4); Jane in *Daylight Robbery II* (ITV) and Fiona Armitage in *Snap* (two series - ITV). Seroca was the voice of Amber in *Star Maths* (three series), directed by Trevor Wywan (Channel 4). She has been a participant on a Director's Course for Talkback Thames' *The Bill*.

GLENN HODGE
Ryan

Glenn trained at
The Arts Educational
School, where his roles
included Wocky in *The
Baby*, Hollarcut in *The
Sea*, Macduff
in *Macbeth* and Astrov in *Uncle
Vanya*. Since graduating in 2004 he
has filmed a leading role in *Murphy's
Law*. *Little Sweet Thing* marks
Glenn's professional
theatre début.

MARCEL MCCALLA
Kev

Marcel played Danny in
the film *Rehab* produced
for the BBC by Ruth
Caleb and Marcel in *The
Big Finish* (The Picture
Company). On
television he has appeared in
Footballers' Wives (Series 3 & 4 -
Shed Productions) as Noah
Alexander; in *Grange Hill* (BBC); in
The Bill (Carlton) as Stevie; in *My
Wonderful Life* (ITV) and in *Mr Charity*
(BBC). On stage Marcel has
appeared as Simon in *The One With
The Oven* (Royal Court); as Emil in
Fallout by Roy Williams (Royal Court
Upstairs); as Artful Dodger in *Oliver
Twist* (Sam Mendes - London
Palladium) and in John Mortimer's
Naked Justice.

ASHLEY MADEKWE
Angela

Ashley is currently in her
final year at R.A.D.A. and
this is her first
professional theatre
production. Roles
played at R.A.D.A.
include Anna Petrovna in *Wild Honey*,
Katherine/Boy in *Henry V*, Katherine
Earnshaw in *Wuthering Heights*,
Pompiona in *The Knight of The
Burning Pestle* and
Phillipinne/Ragamuffin in *On The
Razzle*. She played Annalisa in the
film *Storm Damage*. Television roles
include Bev in *Teachers* (series 1 & 2)
and Janey in *The Bill* and, on radio,
Nicky in *Tell Tale* by Roy Williams.

LAUREN TAYLOR
Zoë

Lauren trained at The
Poor School and has
appeared on television
as Kimberley in *Tunnel of
Love* (Freemantle
Thames). Drama school
productions include Emma Hamilton
in *Bequest to the Nation*, Elida in
Lady from the Sea, Florence in *The
Vortex*, Masha in *The Seagull*, The
Princess in *Sweet Bird Of Youth*,
Lucius/Lepidus in *Julius Caesar* and
Lady Teazle in *School For Scandal*.

ROY WILLIAMS
Writer

Roy's theatre credits include *Sing Yer Heart Out for the Lads (National Theatre); Souls* (Theatre Centre); *The Gift* (Birmingham Rep); *Local Boy* (Hampstead Theatre); *Lift Off, Clubland* and *Fallout* (Royal Court Theatre); *Starstruck* (Tricycle Theatre); *No Boys Cricket Club* (Theatre Royal Stratford East); *Josie's Boys* (Red Ladder Theatre Company) and *Night & Day* (Theatre Venture). For television, he has written *Offside* and *Babyfather* (BBC TV). Roy won the 31st John Whiting Award, the Alfred Fagon Award 1997 and in 1999 an EMMA award for *Starstruck*. He won the George Devine Award 2000 for *Lift Off*, the 2001 Evening Standard Award for Most Promising Playwright for *Clubland*, a 2002 BAFTA Best Schools Drama Award for *Offside*, the 2003 Evening Standard Award nomination for Best Play for *Fallout* and in 2004 the South Bank Show Arts Council Decibel Award for *Fallout*.

MICHAEL BUFFONG
Director

Michael's previous directing credits include *Six Degrees of Separation* (Main House) and *On My Birthday* (Studio) at the Royal Exchange Theatre in Manchester; *Long Time No See* (Talawa Theatre Company); *Raising The Roof* (Shaftesbury Theatre); *Souls* (Theatre Centre); *The Prayer* (Young Vic); *Stories From Mean Street* (New End Theatre Hampstead); *Unfinished Business* (Oval House); *Airport 2000 - Asians In Transit* (Leicester Haymarket/Riverside Studios); *Brother2Brother* (Lyric Hammersmith) and *Scrape Off The Black* (Theatre Royal Stratford East). Television and film credits include *Casualty* and *EastEnders* (BBC) and *Blazed* (C4). Michael has also written and directed the award-winning short film *Simple!*

RUARI MURCHISON
Designer

Ruari has designed productions at The Stratford Festival (Canada), Washington DC, Stuttgart (Germany), Luzern (Switzerland), Haarlem (Holland). London work includes productions at The Royal National Theatre, Royal Court, Greenwich, Soho Theatre, Hampstead and The Young Vic. He has also worked at The Royal Shakespeare Company, Nottingham Playhouse, West Yorkshire Playhouse, Clwyd Theatr Cymru, Birmingham Rep and Bristol Old Vic. Designs include: *Mappa Mundi, Frozen, The Waiting Room, The Red Balloon* (National Theatre); *Titus Andronicus* (Royal Shakespeare Company); *A Busy Day* (Lyric, Shaftesbury Avenue); *Peggy Sue Got Married* (Shaftesbury Theatre); *The Snowman* (Peacock); *West Side Story* and *The Sound of Music* (Stratford Festival, Canada); *Henry IV parts 1 and 2* (Washington DC); *Hamlet* (Birmingham Rep, National Tour and Elisnore, Denmark); *A Doll's House* (National Tour); *Peter Grimes, Cosi fan Tutte* (Luzerner Opera); *La Cenerentola, Il Barbiere di Siviglia* (Garsington); *The Protecting Veil* (Birmingham Royal Ballet); *Landschaft und Erinnerung* (Stuttgart Ballett). His designs for *Racing Demon, The Absence of War* and *Murmuring Judges* at Birmingham Rep were nominated for the TMA Best Design award in 2003.

KAT
Choreographer

Kat B is best known for his antics on *MTV Base, The Lick Parties* (with Trevor Nelson) and the *Request Shows*, in *Aiya Napa, Afro Hair, Beauty* and the well talked about show *Kat in Jamaica*. Kat has appeared in numerous productions at the Theatre Royal, Stratford East including Lorca's *The Public, The Dragon Can't Dance* as well as many variety nights. He also worked as a choreographer on the Theatre Royal's touring musical *One Dance Will Do, Don't Mess With The Controls, The Oddest Couple* and the 2002 production of *Shoot 2 Win*. Other theatre credits include the Scarecrow in *The Wiz* (Hackney Empire); Billy Goose in *Mother Goose* (Hackney Empire); *The Day The Bronx Died* (Tricycle Theatre) and work with The Posse and the Bibi Crew. Kat has also set up and continues to run *Ruff Stuff*, an award-winning dance troupe, and is a regular face to the comedy show *Blaggers*. He's also appeared in Angie Le Mar's *Funny Black Women*. Film and television credits include *Waterland, Street Wise, Up Late With Gina Yashere* (BBC2), *Nights Out At The Empire* (C4) and *The Richard Blackwood Show* (C4). Most recently Kat was seen in *Da Boyz*, a hip-hop musical at the Theatre Royal, Stratford East. Catch Kat with his partner in comedy, Richard Blackwood every Saturday and Sunday, 12pm to 3pm on Choice FM.

RENNY KRUPINSKI
Fight Director

Renny Krupinski is a British Equity Registered Fight Director, director, award-winning actor and writer. Theatre fights include: RSC, Clwyd Theatr Cymru, Royal Exchange & Library Theatre Manchester, Abbey Dublin, Lyric Belfast, Liverpool Everyman & Playhouse, Young Vic, *Les Misérables* (1st UK tour, Germany, Belgium); Leicester Haymarket, West Yorkshire Playhouse Birmingham Rep, Sheffield Crucible, Oldham Coliseum. TV fights include: *The Bill, City Central, Elidor, A&E, Emmerdale, Brookside, Hollyoaks, Peak Practice* and all the violence for *Coronation Street* over the past three years. Television acting includes: *A Touch of Frost, The Falkland's Play, Beech Is Back, City Central, Elidor, Just Us, Silent Witness*, voice & face

of *Oblivion @* Alton Towers and the cult villain Sizzler in *Brookside*. Theatre includes: Salieri /*Adadeus* (twice), Capulet/ *Romeo & Juliet*, Banquo/*Macbeth*, Launcelot Gobbo/*Merchant of Venice*. Directing includes: *Bare, Romeo & Juliet, Comedy of Errors, Titus Andronicus, Katie Crowder, Arabian Nights & Lady Macbeth Rewrites The Rulebook*. Writing includes: *Bare* (Mobil Playwriting Award); *D'Eon*; *Katie Crowder*; *Lady Macbeth Rewrites The Rulebook*; 3 years on *The Bill* and many BBC Radio comedies.

MALCOLM RIPPETH
Lighting Designer

Malcolm studied Drama at the University of Hull. Theatre includes: *The Bacchae, Pandora's Box* (Kneehigh Theatre); *The Lion, the Witch and the Wardrobe, Vodou Nation, Homage to Catalonia, Medea, Off Camera* (West Yorkshire Playhouse); *Kaput!, Cinzano, Smirnova's Birthday, The Snow Queen, Noir, The Tiger's Bride* (Northern Stage); *Toast, Charlie's Trousers, Dirty Nets, Cooking with Elvis* (Live Theatre, Newcastle); *Romeo and Juliet, John Gabriel Borkman* (English Touring Theatre); *Foyer, The Selfish Giant* (Leicester Haymarket); *Dealer's Choice* (Salisbury Playhouse); *Macbeth* (York Theatre Royal); *Keepers of the Flame* (RSC / Live Theatre); *Black Cocktail* (Edinburgh Festival); *Bintou* (Arcola); *Abyssinia* (Tiata Fahodzi); *Tear from a Glass Eye* (Gate / NT Studio). Dance includes: *La Vie des Fantasmes Érotiques et Esthétiques, The Ball* (balletLORENT). Opera includes: *Who Put Bella in the Wych-Elm?, Infinito Nero, Scenes from a Novel* (Almeida Aldeburgh Opera).

AL ASHFORD
Sound Designer

Al started off in theatre as the trainee at the Wolsey in 1992 whilst studying sound at the City of Westminster

College in London. Some of his favourite sound work includes *Ion, The Triumph of Love, To Kill a Mockingbird, Road, Happy Days* (Mercury Theatre, Colchester); *Abena's Stupidest Mistake* (Talawa Theatre Company); *Aladdin, Robin Hood and the Babes in the Wood, Blithe Spirit, Blues For Mr Charlie, Cinderella, Double Indemnity, Foreign Lands, How the Other Half Loves, Road, The Diary of Anne Frank, The Turn of The Screw, Company* and mixing *Sweeney Todd, The Demon Barber of Fleet Street* (Wolsey Theatre and New Wolsey Theatre); 1996 production of *Double Indemnity* (Clwyd Theatr Cymru); *Cinderella* (Hackney Empire); *Mack And Mabel* (The Ipswich Regent); *David Copperfield, The Wuffings, The Timelords of Tacket Street, Tithe War!, Parson Combs And The Ballad of Mad Dog Creek and Boudicca's Babes* (Eastern Angles). Television work includes two series of *It's A Knockout* and lots of boring awards ceremonies. Current projects include the building and running of a new valve and digital based recording studio. Al once worked as a technician in a circus but ended up being a clown.

CLAUDETTE WILLIAMS
Voice Coach

Claudette teaches on the BA Acting course at the Central School of Speech and Drama.

STEVE MARMION
Assistant Director

Steve's work as a director includes productions at the National Theatre, Royal Court Theatre, Theatre Royal Plymouth, Stephen Joseph Theatre Scarborough, Sherman Theatre Cardiff, Edinburgh Festival and numerous national tours. Steve lectures in theatre, directing and education at the Central School of Speech and Drama and at East 15 Acting School. He recently won the London One Act Theatre Festival with his acclaimed production of *Madam Butterfly's Child*. Productions include: *Miranda's Magic Mirror* (Stephen Joseph Theatre, Alan Ayckbourn); *Team Spirit* (Lyttleton National Theatre, Judy Upton); Assistant Director on *Country Music* (Royal Court Theatre, Simon Stephens); *SK8* (Theatre Royal Plymouth, Gary Owen); *More Than Just A Game* (Theatre Royal Plymouth, Larry Alan) and *97 - Hillsborough* (Edinburgh and tour).

The producers would like to thank the following organisations and individuals who have generously supported the production and promotion of *Little Sweet Thing:*

Flava Urban Clothing Fashion, 50 St Matthews Street, Ipswich

Julian Smith

The Link

MK News, Food & Wine Newsagents

Salentina Pizzeria Ristorante

Stoke High School, Ipswich

Little Sweet Thing

Characters

Kev, *late teens, black*
Tash, *mid-teens, black*
Zoë, *mid-teens, white*
Nathan, *mid-teens, white*
Miss Jules, *early thirties, black*
Ryan, *late teens, white*
Jamal, *late teens, mixed race*
Angela, *late teens, mixed race*
'The Hood'

Act One

Enter **Kev**.

Kev *is alone onstage. He is playing basketball, shooting hoops. It starts off very light, relaxed, but then becomes faster and furious.* **Kev** *plays like a man possessed. The more hoops he misses, the more frustrated he gets.*

Kev *stops to take a breath. He turns to find a hooded teenager, with his face obscured, watching him.* **Kev** *stares back. He is not surprised to see him there. The* **Hood** *picks up the ball and gestures to* **Kev**, *offering a game of one-on-one.* **Kev**, *looking a little frightened, walks away. The hooded teenager just laughs.*

Exit **Kev**.

Exit the **Hood**.

Enter **Tash**, **Nathan** *and* **Zoë**.

Zoë Giss it, Tash.

Tash (*reads*) 'Kian, how old were you when you had your first kiss, and were you scared? Lots of love, Jackie from Edinburgh.'

Zoë Giss it.

Tash Well, Jackie . . .

Zoë Juss giss it . . .

Tash I suppose I should say I was all hard and macho, and say that it was amazing. It was with a girl at school who was so cute, and I was so nervous, both of us were waiting for the other to make the first move, but I think I've improved since then. I was eleven. Oh man!

Zoë Can I have my magazine back now?

Tash No.

Zoë Tash?

Tash 'Dear Kian, how sensitive are you? Clare from Bristol.' Well, Clare, my best friend Jason calls me Mr Sensitivity, cos he thinks I'm sensitive and I have no problems showing it. I'm always very passionate about how I feel. (*Laughs.*) Oh, shame.

Zoë Alright, so you don't like Westlife.

Tash I'd piss on Westlife.

Zoë So giss it back.

Tash *drops it.*

Tash Well, pick it up.

Zoë *bends down.* **Tash** *kicks the magazine away.*

Tash Sorry.

Zoë *leans over.* **Tash** *kicks it away again.*

Tash Really sorry.

Zoë *walks away.*

Tash Where you going?

Zoë Home.

Tash You got detention, fool.

Zoë Don't care.

Tash So pick up yer mag.

Zoë You're gonna kick it away again.

Tash No I won't.

Zoë Don't want it now.

Tash Pick it up.

Zoë *leans over.* **Tash** *does it again.*

Tash Really, really sorry. (*Hears* **Zoë** *mumbling.*) Yeah, who you cussing like that?

Zoë I weren't cussing.

Tash (*laughs*) Zoë Bishop, think she turn bad now.

Zoë I ain't afraid of you.

Tash You should be.

Zoë Cos you hang round with Donna.

Tash I don't hang round with Donna no more.

Zoë Why?

Tash She's a ho.

Zoë Least she don't pick on me.

Tash She nicks yer money, you fool.

Zoë So she doesn't pick on me.

Tash Soff.

Zoë Fine, I'm soff.

Tash Believe.

Zoë So leave me alone.

Tash I'll leave you alone when I feel like leaving you alone.

Zoë *quickly swipes up the magazine from the ground.*

Tash (*mocks*) Westlife! They can't even sing.

Zoë Can! I saw them on *Top of the Pops*, singing live.

Tash You sad cow.

Zoë So what are you?

Tash What am I?

Zoë If I'm sad, you're even sadder for bothering me.

Tash Stop pretending.

Zoë Bout what?

Tash   I know you're afraid of me. I can see it.

Zoë   Alright, I'm afraid of you.

Tash   Are you taking the piss, Zoë?

Zoë   No.

Tash   I'll cut your throat out.

Zoë   I said I'm scared, you've got me shaking.

Tash   Get out of my face.

Zoë   Can't.

Tash   You can't?

Zoë   We're in detention.

Tash   Bloody Westlife.

Zoë   Yeah, you hate them.

Tash   Everyone knows they're splitting up.

Zoë   No.

Tash   Read it in the paper.

Zoë   You read about Westlife?

Tash   They're everywhere, hard not to.

Zoë   No it ain't. Just turn the page.

Tash   You really love being clever, ennit? You best not try that with Donna. She'll cut yer tongue out.

Zoë   Thanks for the warning.

Tash   Move. (*Eyes* **Nathan**.) So what?

Nathan   What?

Tash   You can't talk?

Nathan   Yes.

Tash   That was a wicked goal you got against St George's.

Nathan   Yeah, I know.

Tash   Is it true, then?

Nathan   What's true?

Tash   You playing for Arsenal.

Nathan   I don't know yet.

Tash   But they want to see you.

Nathan   Yeah, but I still don't know.

Tash   You gonna go Highbury? Meet Thierry Henry? I'm coming with you, yeah. It'll be my birthday soon, that'll be my present. I have to meet Thierry Henry, yeah, yeah?

Nathan   Maybe. Why you looking at me like that?

Tash   Like what?

Nathan   Like that.

Tash   I ain't looking at you any way, white boy, so shut up! I'm just asking you a question.

Nathan   Yeah.

Tash   Ejut.

Enter **Miss Jules**.

Tash   Can I go now, Miss?

Miss Jules   And miss out on all the fun we're going to have together?

Tash   Chat is dry.

Miss Jules   I'm surprised to see you here, Zoë, what's going on?

Zoë   Fighting.

Miss Jules   You were fighting?

Tash   I know, I can't believe it either, her fight?

Miss Jules   Hey.

Tash   What?

Miss Jules   Quiet. Nathan?

Nathan   Weren't my fault.

Miss Jules   Why do you children love to say that?

Nathan   Mr Cotton put me on the subs bench for the game against Newton, cos he didn't like my attitude.

Miss Jules   Do you have one?

Nathan   No, I just like winning. Mr Cotton don't, he's useless. Bring back Mr Singh. He wouldn't listen to what I'm saying, playing three up front is mad, midfield is having a hard time holding the ball as it is, told him nuff times, he blanks me, so, I goes, 'Excuse me, sir, but did you drop these?' (*Raises two fingers.*) 'Or was it this?' (*Gives the finger.*)

Tash   Like it.

Nathan   He didn't.

Miss Jules   What did you expect?

Tash   Ain't you gonna ask me?

Miss Jules   I don't need to ask. You love up detention.

Tash   Like you love up Mr Denning. I've seen you with him.

Miss Jules   Does my face look like I'm in the mood for this?

Tash   Can't take it, don't dish it out.

Miss Jules   Alright, listen, none of us wants to be here, so let's get it over with, now. Now, what can I do?

Tash   Let us go.

Miss Jules   You know what, when I was about your age, I saw this film about a teacher who was running a detention for a group of kids all day Saturday.

Tash Detention on Saturday?

Miss Jules Yes.

Tash All the kids went?

Miss Jules Yes.

Tash They spases or what? Was it a special-needs school or summin?

Miss Jules Natasha?

Tash Saturday? Nossir! The only place you finding me on Saturday morning is in my bed.

Miss Jules May I finish?

Tash Gwan den.

Miss Jules Thank you.

Tash Yer welcome.

Miss Jules This teacher –

Tash What was his name?

Miss Jules This teacher decided to try something new with these kids, he had each of them write an essay, a thousand words I think, describing to him who they think they are and what brought them to detention in the first place.

Tash Seen.

Miss Jules So that is what I would like you to do. One essay please, each. Who you are, what do you want. Begin.

Tash So what happened at the end of the film, Miss?

Miss Jules They all realised how foolish they were, said sorry to the teacher and went about their way.

Zoë You're wrong, Miss.

Tash Oh yes!

Miss Jules Just get on with it, Zoë, please.

Zoë   You're wrong.

Miss Jules   Zoë?

Tash   So what did happen?

Zoë   All the kids got together, reckoned the teacher was an arsehole, so they write one joint letter, I've seen the film, it was on Living TV.

Tash   Oh shame, Miss.

Miss Jules   Thank you, Zoë.

Tash   Why didn't you want us to know that?

Miss Jules   Get on with it, Natasha.

Tash   Miss get vex!

Miss Jules   This is detention. I don't want to hear nothing but silence, from now on.

Tash   So moany.

Miss Jules   Now on!

Exit **Tash**, **Miss Jules**, **Zoë** *and* **Nathan**.

Enter **Ryan** *and* **Jamal**.

Ryan   I'm sorry, Jamal, can you repeat that?

Jamal   You deaf?

Ryan   Yes, I must be. Ca fer a minute deh, I coulda swore you said no.

Jamal   I did say no.

Ryan   No you didn't.

Jamal   Ryan, beg you, don't piss around wid me please, not today.

Ryan   Awright then, I won't.

Jamal   Thank you.

Ryan Juss gimme a little summin.

Jamal Bwoi.

Ryan I go, I be on my way.

Jamal In case it has escaped that mash-up dirty smelly head of yours, I provided you with a little summin last week but what you ain't coming up with is dollars, dough, pieces of paper with the Queen's face on it. You get me?

Ryan Yeah, man, I got you.

Jamal I mean, did someone change my name to soff without telling me?

Ryan I gotta go, blood.

Jamal Good. Now tek yer arse home with you.

Ryan You go sort me out?

Jamal Nigga deaf!

Ryan Blood.

Jamal What did I say to you?

Ryan Come.

Jamal Whoa, step back, move back five paces.

Ryan What you say?

Jamal Do it now.

Ryan What I do?

Jamal You never hear of soap?

Ryan Jamal, man. It's me. Ryan. Relay team.

Jamal Don't start with that.

Ryan Go, Compton, go!

Jamal Alright, man. Just don't start with that. Please.

Ryan *starts running.*

Jamal   Please!

Jamal *hands him some rocks.*

Ryan   Nice.

Jamal   Wass that smile for?

Ryan   You know me, I always smile.

Jamal   Don't fleece me. Ryan.

Ryan   Would I . . .

Jamal   Don't do it.

Ryan   Blood.

Jamal   Go wash yourself.

Exit **Jamal**.

Enter **Kev**. *He flicks the back of* **Ryan**'s *ear.*

Kev   Yer too ugly!

Ryan (*delighted*)   Oh shit!

Kev   Tek yer hand off my arse, please.

Ryan   When you get out?

Kev   This morning.

Ryan   What, you couldn't bell me?

Kev   I bin inside for months, they probably cut me off.

Ryan   I'll get you a new phone.

Kev   It's alright.

Ryan   Gotta march you off to KFC, blood, you lose weight. Gotta get yer sack emptied.

Kev   Empty your own. I knew I'd find you out here.

Ryan   Where else?

Kev   Bredren, you stink, man.

Ryan   Yeah yeah, never mind that. I'm glad you're here, bro.

Kev   Why?

Ryan   Jamal. Bwoi thinks his man now. Top shotter. You gotta tek him, Kev, get your throne back, believe!

Kev   I just got out, Ryan.

Ryan   Then it's me and you, you and me, me and you.

Kev   Are you listening to me?

Ryan   Like it was to begin with.

Kev   Slow down.

Ryan   Going rave tomorrow night, you coming?

Kev   Ain't bin home yet.

Ryan   What you waiting for?

Kev   Don't even know if my mum wants me deh.

Ryan   She better, ca you ain't bringing yourself round my yard.

Kev   Why, yer mum still love me up?

Ryan   Your gran loves me up.

Kev   Yer mum was grinding me for so long, I grew an afro.

Ryan (*laughs*)   Missed this.

Kev   Missed this too.

Enter **Tash**.

Tash   Yeah, I thought I'd find you two hugging each other.

Kev   LST!

Tash   Batty bwois, dass you two.

Kev   Come here.

Tash   Wat you doing?

Kev   Gonna tump you up.

Tash *thumps her brother on her arm.*

Kev   Ow!

Tash   What you doing out?

Kev   I told you.

Tash   Next week, you said.

Kev   Well, I'm here now.

Tash   You ain't having your room back.

Kev   Did I ask?

Tash   You ain't having it.

Kev   I don't have to ask, I'm juss gonna take it.

Tash   No, you ain't gonna juss take it.

Ryan   Mouth, big bwoi.

Tash   What you staring at?

Ryan   Nuttin.

Kev *gives* **Ryan** *a little shove as if to say 'Don't look at my sister like that'.*

Kev   Mum know you dress like that?

Tash   Yes.

Kev   Lie.

Tash   Lend me some dollars. I'm broke.

Kev   My problem how? Don't even get a hug, shit like that.

Tash *(hugs him)*   Missed yer, bro.

Ryan   You have one for me?

Tash   Gway! Mum know yer back?

Kev   How can she know if you didn't know?

Tash   You best call her. Can't just show up, give her a stroke.

Kev   Pass yer phone.

Ryan *hands* **Kev** *his phone.*

Exit **Kev**.

Ryan   You alright?

Tash   Yes.

Ryan   Still raving?

Tash   Maybe.

Ryan   Going emporium?

Tash   Whenever I feel.

Ryan   At yer age. Kev know?

Tash   You best not tell him. Stop looking at me.

Ryan   Why?

Tash   Ca yer nasty.

Ryan   Shush.

Tash   Fraid he'll hear?

Ryan   Still look nice.

Tash   You ain't getting none.

Ryan   Weren't too shy a month ago.

Tash   That was then, could have you arrested.

Ryan   You didn't push me away.

Tash   I'm sorry, but are you under the impression that something happened then?

Ryan   Didn't it?

Tash   You get points for trying, though. Really trying.

Ryan   Bitch.

Tash   Kev?

Ryan   Chill. You love to tease.

Enter **Kev**.

Kev   She wants me home. You as well.

Tash   Why you tell her I was with you?

Kev   Shut up and come.

Tash   So moany.

Ryan   I come fer you at ten tomorrow, yeah? Rave?

Kev   Dunno, Ryan.

Ryan   Quiet.

Tash   Yes, Kev, quiet.

Ryan   Yer coming.

Exit **Ryan**.

Tash   A guy is sitting by a window, which he desperately wants to open. But he knows if he does, it will kill him. Why?

Kev   Guy by a window . . .

Tash   Yeah?

Kev   . . . wants to open window but it'll kill him . . .

Tash   Yeah yeah, get to it.

Kev   Is he on a bus?

Tash   How can opening a bus window kill you?

Kev   I dunno.

Tash Ejut.

Kev Tell me.

Tash It's so easy.

Kev Tell me.

Exit **Kev**.

Enter **Miss Jules**.

Tash Are you gonna move, Miss?

Miss Jules No.

Tash Just move.

Miss Jules Take a breath.

Tash I don't want to take a breath, I want to go out there and take Donna's head off, you don't think I can, I can. See how she mess up my hair. What, what you staring at?

Miss Jules A young man reaches a crossroads in the middle of a deserted road.

Tash Look, I ain't in the mood for one of your dry puzzles, yeah.

Miss Jules Calm down.

Tash Step out of the way.

Miss Jules You used to enjoy them.

Tash When I was twelve. Do I look twelve to you?

Miss Jules Alright then.

Tash Thank you.

Miss Jules If you're too soft to work it out.

Tash Soft?

Miss Jules Soft! (*Spells.*) S-O-F-T.

Tash Don't go there, Miss.

Miss Jules   So stop me. Come on. Donna ain't going nowhere.

Tash   Alright, hit me with it.

Miss Jules   A young man reaches a crossroads in the middle of the road. Standing there, between the roads, is a very old man. One road leads to the most beautiful town in the world, where everyone is warm and friendly and always tells the truth. The other leads to a nasty beat-up town, where everyone is horrible to each other, always tells lies and is a cannibal. (*Plays being a cannibal.*)

Tash (*unimpressed*)   Don't give up your day job.

Miss Jules   The young man wants to go to the nice town. The old man could come from either one of those towns, but he is only capable of answering one question. What question does the young man ask to find his way to the nice town?

Tash   An old man?

Miss Jules   Yes.

Tash   One town full of nice people who always tell the truth, the other full of cannibals who lie all the time?

Miss Jules   Yes, get to it.

Tash   'Which way is it to your town?' That's what he asks. He goes whichever way the guy is pointing.

Miss Jules   Explain.

Tash   If he's a liar, he's going to point in the opposite direction of his town. If he's telling the truth, he's gonna point same way. Both answers lead the same way. Don't waste my time, Miss.

Miss Jules   I've told you this one before.

Tash   No.

Miss Jules   I don't know anyone who got it that quickly. I didn't.

Tash   Ca yer soft.

Miss Jules   Soft?

Tash   S-O-F-T. Now if you don't mind, I'd like to go back out there and finish stamping on Donna's head.

Miss Jules   Sit yourself down.

Tash   You promised.

Miss Jules   I didn't promise you that, be quiet. I thought you two were mates.

Tash   Donna's a bitch.

Miss Jules   Hey!

Tash   Carrying on like her shit don't stink.

Miss Jules   That's enough.

Tash   Claiming that Jason is her man. Is it my fault he can't keep his eyes off me? I don't think so.

Miss Jules   You must have done something to make him look.

Tash   All I do is smile, I like to smile.

Miss Jules   At boys.

Tash   We were in the hallway, having a good time, she goes menstrual on me.

Miss Jules   Why?

Tash   Cos she's a mad cow like her mum.

Miss Jules   Tash!

Tash   It's true. I was only playing him along, work him up a sweat, then blow him out.

Miss Jules   Do you know what that makes you sound like?

Tash   I can handle it.

Miss Jules   I bet that's what Naomi said about Derek.

Tash (*chuckles*)   You tink I go let some boy rape me? I'll kill him first. You shoulda seen her face, man, sayin I bin trying to take Jason away from her. I goes, I don't need to try, love, I don't need to do anything, except keep looking this good. Look at him, look at how big his beast is growing already. He do that for you?

Miss Jules   His beast?

Tash   You know what I mean by beast, don't you, Miss?

Miss Jules   Yes, thank you.

Tash   She says she's gonna get her big brother to sort me out, I says I'll get my brother to shoot her brother in the face, then yer mama's face.

Miss Jules   That is an awful thing to say.

Tash   I was scaring her. Mr Denning shouldn't have pulled me off, I was up for killing her.

Miss Jules   Natasha?

Tash   What, man?

Miss Jules   Stop it.

Tash   You wanted to know.

Miss Jules   Just remember who you're talking to.

Tash *sucks her teeth.*

Miss Jules   Do you want to get excluded? Keep it up.

Tash   Typical.

Miss Jules   Excuse me?

Tash   One minute you're down wid us, next you're barking orders at us like the rest of the teachers.

Miss Jules   I am not *down* with any of you.

Tash   Well, step out of way, then.

Miss Jules Do you really like this Jason? Or is he just something to pass away the time?

Tash Ain't my fault there's nuttin else to do.

Miss Jules There is plenty for you to do.

Tash Why do you care so much?

Miss Jules Why shouldn't I? Don't waste any more time on this boy – who am I calling a boy – he's a grown man –

Tash He's only twenty.

Miss Jules   – who spends half his time hanging round school gates with his brers.

Tash *laughs*.

Miss Jules What?

Tash The way you try to chat like us sometimes, it's funny.

Miss Jules What Jason is doing, listen to me, is not funny. It's nastiness.

Tash Is this Miss Jules, teacher, talking?

Miss Jules Yes it is. What do you expect?

Tash You want to stand like the rest of them. You're no better than me. Don't you get bored?

Miss Jules Every day.

Tash So why do it?

Miss Jules Because no one else will, that's what I'm trying to say to you –

Tash See, deh you go again.

Miss Jules Alright, fine, you know what, I'll shut up.

Tash Thank you.

Miss Jules From now on.

Tash Good.

Miss Jules I'm shutting up.

Tash So hurry up.

Miss Jules But when I'm miles away from here, Tash –

Tash Jeez –

Miss Jules – you'll find out.

Tash What you mean, miles? You ain't leaving. Are you?

Miss Jules Will you miss me?

Tash No.

Miss Jules Because I'm just another teacher.

Tash Because you ain't going. Are you?

Miss Jules No.

Tash Cool.

Miss Jules So what about you, don't you get bored?

Tash You with your questions.

Miss Jules Well?

Tash I dunno.

Miss Jules 'Well, dunno was made to know.'

Tash What?

Miss Jules It's something my mother used to say.

Tash They've always got things to say, mums, ennit?

Miss Jules Believe.

Tash *smiles.*

Miss Jules What, don't you lot say that now?

Tash No, you're alright, it was good. Can I go now please?

Miss Jules   No more fighting?

Tash   No more fighting.

Miss Jules   Promise me.

Tash   I promise, bwoi man.

Miss Jules   Was that a real promise?

Tash   What do you think?

Miss Jules   Natasha?

Tash   What?

Miss Jules   You're too good for this.

Tash   Chill out, Miss.

Exit **Tash** *and* **Miss Jules**.

Enter **Kev** *and* **Angela**.

Angela *links arms with a startled* **Kev**.

Angela   Alright, babes?

Kev   What?

Angela *grabs his face and gives him a huge kiss on the lips.*

Kev (*dazed*)   What?

Angela   Brandy and Coke, please.

Kev (*still dazed*)   What?

Angela   Drink, ennit.

Kev   What?

Angela (*whispers*)   Will you just get me a drink please . . . ?

Kev (*coming to*)   Who are you?

Angela   Yer my man, ennit, yer good for me.

Angela *embraces him. She looks up and waves at somebody.*

Angela   Bye. (*Releases* **Kev**.) Finally.

Kev   What you chatting about?

Angela   Some guy over deh. All I did was smile at him, and all night I can't shake him off.

Kev   Maybe you shouldn't smile so much.

Angela   Maybe he shouldn't be such a dog. Anyhow, thanks anyway.

Kev   You want a drink?

Angela   Oh, please.

Kev   What?

Angela   Gimme summin new, man.

Kev   You came to me.

Angela   Why you niggas have to be the same?

Kev   A drink. That was all I said.

Angela   You think I don't know?

Kev   No.

Angela   I know.

Kev   Bye then.

Exit **Angela**.

Enter **Jamal**.

Jamal   Trying to sharpen your pencil, Kev?

Kev   You call that a cuss, Jamal?

Jamal   So where she go?

Kev   Cut it loose. She's one of them tight-arsed mixed-raced girls. Too much chat.

Jamal   You lose weight.

Kev   Why does everybody have to ask that?

Jamal   Calm yerself.

Kev   I am calm.

Jamal   So what's this I hear?

Kev   Depends?

Jamal   Bout you.

Kev   Don't be shy.

Jamal   Got a job working in supermarket?

Kev   What of it?

Jamal   Gupta's! So it's true.

Kev   How you know?

Jamal   Kieron see you putting out rubbish for him. You know how long he was laughing for?

Kev   So?

Jamal   You go tek that? A year ago, you would have buss Kieron's head for smiling at you. Is this a career move?

Kev   It's a job.

Jamal   It's a liberty. How much dough you on?

Kev   Ain't about the dough. I need summin to do.

Jamal   Come with me, I got plenty for you to do.

Kev   Ah, so yer running tings now?

Jamal   Believe.

Kev   Did you have plenty for Marcus's little brother to do? I heard.

Jamal   Accident.

Kev   He got stabbed.

Jamal   He knew what he was doing.

Kev   He's fifteen.

Jamal   Yeah, I know how old he is. Thank you.

Kev   I was sexing Clare Joseph when I was fifteen.

Jamal   Every boy in that school was sexing Clare Joseph.
Except Ryan.

Kev   Now thass cold.

Jamal   But true.

Kev   Yeah.

Jamal   Tell you what else I was doing. Winning the relay
race.

Kev   No, we won the relay race.

Jamal   Excuse me, who ran past the finishing line first?

Kev   Excuse me, who passed the baton to you?

Jamal   Who made up time cos Ryan slipped up?

Kev   Marcus.

Jamal   Me.

Kev   Marcus! St George's had the race nearly won by then,
I never see a boy run so fast.

Jamal   Alright, it was Marcus., But it was me one everyone
lifted up on their shoulders, carrying around cheering.
Remember that.

Kev   You could never shut up about it.

Jamal's *phone rings. He answers.*

Jamal (*to phone*)   Don't bother me.

Jamal *hangs up.*

Kev   Nice.

Jamal   The finest. I can download music, ring tones, make
a little film, can you believe that?

Kev   Prim and proper, Jamal.

Jamal   Just telling you how it is. Our man says hello.

Kev   He's your man now.

Jamal   He says any time you want –

Kev   No.

Jamal   I'm just relaying the message.

Kev   Not happening.

Jamal   You really mean that?

Kev   Would I say it if I didn't?

Jamal   Ca you know I'm top-shotter now.

Kev   You hear what I said?

Jamal   Yer my brer, I love you to death, but don't just think I'm gonna step aside now, yeah . . .

Kev   Jamal, chill.

Jamal   This new you is gonna take some getting used to boy. And Ryan don't mind?

Kev   Ryan don't matter. You want him, take him.

Jamal   Nuh, you keep him. Only time that fool wants me is when he wants to get high. And I'm sure he's fleecing me, I don't know how yet.

Kev   No.

Jamal   See, deh you go.

Kev   What?

Jamal   Don't go looking after him like you always do.

Kev   I'm not, I'm juss saying Ryan wouldn't do that.

Jamal   Ryan better not be.

Kev   Why are you talking like that? He's our brer.

Jamal   Ease up, might not even come to that.

Kev   Might not?

Jamal   Alright, it won't, so rest. (*Changing the subject.*) Where's your phone?

Kev *shrugs.*

Jamal   You want this one?

Kev   No.

Jamal   Take it. I have three.

Kev   I'm alright.

Jamal   Seen.

Kev   You wanna know where I went as soon as I got out?

Jamal   Get yer sack emptied?

Kev   School.

Jamal   Wa?

Kev   Met Miss Jules, she was going on about me coming back, doing my A levels again.

Jamal   First Gupta's, now school. Gwan, Kev, do yerself proud.

Kev   It took me five minutes before I run outta deh. So rest.

Jamal   Why run?

Kev   The school's still got that funny stale smell in there, all dem boys and yats running round, couldn't move, couldn't breathe. Hearing Miss Jules go on again about us yout wasting ourselves, I goes, 'Listen, yeah, it took everything in me jus to come here, so drop the chat.' She wouldn't, so I stepped. Should never have gone back. You ever feel like going back?

Jamal   School? You mad?

Kev   What we were.

Jamal   Promising students?

The boys laugh.

Soff.

Kev   Could have had different lives.

Jamal   What lives?

Kev   Different lives.

Jamal   Minimum wage in some shop?

Kev (*feeling hurt*)   It was just a question, Jamal.

Jamal   You go work in Gupta's, Kev, till you drop.

Exit **Kev** *and* **Jamal**.

Enter **Tash** *and* **Zoë**.

Tash   Yes? Can I help you?

Zoë   No, I was . . .

Tash   What?

Zoë   Leaving you something, God!

Zoë *hands her a letter.*

Tash   I didn't say you could move.

She opens the letter. It is a card.

(*Reads.*) 'To Tash, thanks for your help, Zoë.' (*To* **Zoë**.) Are you for real?

Zoë   I'm just saying thanks.

Tash   Then say thanks. Don't send me a card. You could get beaten up for summin like that.

Zoë   Won't bother next time.

Tash   There won't be a next time.

Zoë   Why you so horrible? Thought you liked me.

Tash   Who said I liked you?

Zoë   Why save me from Donna?

Tash   Felt like it.

Zoë   She's a cow.

Tash   Say that to her face.

Zoë   Did.

Tash   And that is why you kept running into her fist.

Zoë   Woulda been worse if you hadn't come.

Tash   I didn't do it for you.

Zoë   So why did you?

Tash   She had it coming.

Zoë   Thanks anyway.

Tash   Hey, who told you to move? I'll tell you when you can move.

Zoë   Well, tell me.

Tash   Sorry?

Zoë   When I can move.

Tash (*laughs*)   You're weird. I'm still trying to work you out.

Zoë   Nuttin to work out.

Tash   Why you do it?

Zoë   Do what?

Tash   Act the way you do. I've seen you.

Zoë   Seen me?

Tash   With your silly little white mates. Girly chats. Loving up Westlife.

Zoë   Fancy me, do yer?

Tash (*grabs her*)   Cos all you're doing, yeah, is wearing a big sign on you –

Zoë Let go of me.

Tash – big red letters, saying kick me, hit me, bully me –

Zoë You know you're hurting me.

Tash – cos I'm a sad case.

Zoë Let go.

Tash *releases her.*

Tash You want to stay alive? Cut it out.

Zoë Be like your mates. Act all bad.

Tash We get respect.

Zoë Ain't respect. All the kids are afraid of you. They have to leave their phones at home, in case you lot take them.

Tash I could buss yer head right now, you know that?

Zoë Whatever.

Tash Don't chat back to me.

Zoë OK.

Tash I ain't joking.

Zoë I know.

Tash I mean it.

Zoë Calm down.

Tash You think Donna was bad? I'm twice as bad as her if I get on your arse.

Zoë Kinky.

Tash *grabs her.*

Zoë Get off me.

Tash You're scared, tell me you're scared.

Zoë I'm scared.

Tash *lets her go.*

Tash   Go drool over Westlife.

Zoë   I don't just like Westlife.

Tash   I said go.

Zoë   I like Blue, Beyoncé, Usher.

Tash   Am I supposed to be impressed?

Zoë   See what I mean?

Tash   You have two seconds to disappear.

Zoë   We try to be like you, but you don't want to know, no matter how hard we try.

Tash   Stop your crying.

Zoë   You want to keep us down, gives you something to do. Tracey Wheeler's white. Didn't stop her hanging round with you.

Tash   You ain't Tracey.

Zoë   Wass she got?

Tash   Style.

Zoë   Crap.

Tash   You either have it –

Zoë   You ain't.

Tash   You really want me to buss yer head?

Zoë   You've seen me, I've seen you.

Tash   Explain.

Zoë   The way you laugh and chat. Winding up Miss Jules. But it don't look right. If Donna was here now, she woulda killed me.

Tash   Don't ever think I can't.

Zoë Ain't you bored –

Tash Be quiet.

Zoë – of pretending?

Tash Go.

Zoë I'm going.

Tash Go watch yer Westlife videos.

Zoë I will. I've got their live concert on DVD.

Tash How many times you've seen it?

Zoë Loads. You want to see it?

Tash (*sighs*) Who are you, man? Who do you think you are?

Zoë No one.

Tash What do you think I am?

Zoë You want to see it?

Tash Move.

Zoë See yer tomorrow.

Exit **Zoë**.

Tash *follows* **Zoë**.

Enter **Kev** *and* **Angela**.

Angela How does the sweater feel?

Kev Tight.

Angela I'll ask Gupta to make a badge for you. In the meantime, wear this.

Kev (*reads*) Mohammed?

Angela You look like a Mohammed.

Kev I ain't no Muslim.

Angela   Nor is he. Right, your hours are twelve to six.

Kev   Yeah. I know.

Angela   Your duties are mopping up, cleaning up.

Kev   Look. I've been through this.

Angela   If we short-handed at the front, you'll work the till. Anything we need from the storeroom, you get it for us. You see the shelves?

Kev   Yes.

Angela   You'll be stacking and wiping them.

Kev   Cool.

Angela   Nobody else wants to be here, you know.

Kev   I said I was cool.

Angela   I can see it in yer face.

Kev   Sorry?

Angela   You'll find what you want.

Kev   You don't even know me.

Angela   I didn't when I started here, now I'm going college next month. Here's your mop. Do you even remember me?

Kev   I ain't blind. The rave.

Angela   I hope you ain't stalking me.

Kev   How am I supposed to know you work here?

Angela   You missed a spot.

Kev *sucks his teeth.*

Angela   Excuse me?

Kev   What?

Angela   What was that?

Kev   What was what?

Angela   You just sucked your teeth at me.

Kev   No I didn't.

Angela   Yes you did.

Kev   You must be mistaken.

Angela   Do you want to go on a warning?

Kev   Excuse me, but I got a floor to mop.

Angela   You a bad bwoi. Kev?

Kev   Why, you like them?

Angela   I like men.

Kev *continues to mop.* **Angela** *stares.*

Kev   You want summin?

Angela   A drink.

Kev   Thought you wanted summin new.

Angela   That was last night, catch up.

Kev   Gal, yer fast.

Angela   I ain't no gal.

Kev   You live round here?

Angela   Near enough. You?

Kev *(points)*   See that estate?

Angela   Me as well.

Kev   You a Cleveland gal? Shut up.

Angela   What's your problem?

Kev   Never see you.

Angela   It's a big estate, you think you know every gal?

Kev   Pretty much.

Angela   You didn't know me.

Kev   You said you're no gal. Where did you live?

Angela   Angel House.

Kev (*points at her name tag*)   Like yer name. Angela.

Angela (*smiles*)   Maybe I saw you, maybe not. You bwois are all the same with your chat.

Kev   That ain't me.

Angela   Yeah.

Kev   Well, I'm trying.

Angela   Why try?

Kev   Why ask that?

Angela   Curious.

Kev   Bin away. Yeah?

Angela   Away where? Holiday?

Kev   No, I bin away.

Angela   Where?

Kev   Come on, Angela.

Angela   Come on what?

Kev   You said yer a Cleveland gal.

Angela   So?

Kev   So act like one.

Angela   Mek up noise?

Kev   I've bin in prison, that's what I'm trying to explain to you.

Angela   You couldn't have just said that?

Kev   I'm saying it now. You don't know me.

Angela   Guess not.

Kev   Know you, though. Killing time before college. Living in some flat with your two mates.

Angela   It's three mates.

Kev   I was close.

Angela   Keep trying, Kev.

Exit **Kev**.

Enter **Jamal**.

Angela   So?

Jamal   So?

Angela   How you get in, Jamal?

Jamal   Through the door. Used the key.

Angela   You made a copy?

Jamal   I didn't think you meant what you said last time.

Angela   Gimme dem.

Jamal   Please.

Angela   Jamal, don't piss about, man.

Jamal   You got A levels now, gal. Can't be talking like that.

Angela   Please.

Jamal *throws the keys to her.*

Angela   Is that your car outside?

Jamal   Hold your tongue. Ain't just a car. It's a four-by-four.

Angela   Where you teif it?

Jamal   It's my man's car.

Angela   Oh yes, yer man.

Jamal   You don't think that's summin? Him trusting me wid his car?

Angela   It's summin alright.

Jamal (*shows phone*)   Bought me this, this. You like? Marched me into the store, he did, tell me to pick any phone. I reach for this one, and I goes, 'Oh yes, this is working.' My man paid for it in cash. Ain't cheap, slammed that money down on the counter.

Angela   You sound like a kid with a new toy.

Jamal   So?

Angela   Kinda sweet.

Jamal (*embarrassed*)   Sweet?

Angela   I used to think you were sweet. *Beau garçon.*

Jamal   *Merci.* Come outside for a minute.

Angela   I'm busy.

Jamal   Wid what?

Angela   Getting my head down.

Jamal   Car go like a dream.

Angela   Jamal?

Jamal   Come see.

Angela   No.

Jamal   You'll see.

Angela   I'll tell you what, why don't you go and take one of yer little schoolgirls for a ride?

Jamal   Ca I want to tek you.

Angela   I don't want to go.

Jamal   You used to love tekin rides.

Angela   Not no more.

Jamal   Who you tekin rides from now?

Angela   None of yer business.

Jamal   Right.

Angela   Believe.

Jamal   It's that boy in the shop, ennit?

Angela   What?

Jamal   Just tell me it ain't him.

Angela   What you doing, spying on me?

Jamal   I weren't spying.

Angela   You're everywhere. The rave. My home. Now work.
Cut it out.

Jamal   Oh, calm yerself.

Angela   Leave me.

Jamal   You know how many times Gupta's get robbed,
I don't know why you working in there in the first place.

Angela   I need money.

Jamal   I just like to cruise by every so often, make sure yer
alright.

Angela   I don't need you cruising by for me.

Jamal   Should be thanking me.

Angela   Well, I ain't.

Jamal   Saw you chatting with him. At the rave.

Angela   None of yer business.

Jamal   I know.

Angela   Good.

Jamal   Long as it ain't him.

Angela   He do summin to you?

Jamal   Dunno yet.

Angela   I don't know what's wrong wid you boys.

Jamal   Nuttin wrong wid me.

Angela   What you done now?

Jamal   Hey, it ain't me, it's some little turd I gotta be dealing with now.

Angela   Why?

Jamal   Ca my man says so. Oderwise he's gonna be dealing with me.

Angela   Ahh, after he buy you such a nice phone.

Jamal   No one gives me backchat as good as you. I've missed it.

Angela   I miss Jamal.

Jamal   I don't want to, you nuh. I have to.

Angela   Please, what do you want?

Jamal   Alright, look, yeah, no promises mind, but after much consideration, I'd thought I'd give you another chance.

Angela   Is it?

Jamal   Yes!

Angela   Yer so kind.

Jamal   I know. So, can I?

Angela   What?

Jamal   Move back?

Angela   Of course. Any time. Right now?

Jamal   Cool.

Angela   I'll just be in Manchester.

Jamal You got in?

Angela Yes.

Jamal So what about Brunel? You always chatted about going to Brunel.

Angela I changed my mind.

Jamal And it's now you tell me?

Angela Yes.

Jamal You just gonna pack up and leave?

Angela Yes.

Jamal Bitch.

Angela You catching on now, Jamal.

Jamal Don't come it with yer smart talk.

Angela Take your threats someplace else.

Jamal Everything I say, you take as a threat. Don't look at me like that, like you're scared of me. Please. Manchester?

Angela Yes, Manchester.

Jamal Who go look after you?

Angela Myself. Jamal, don't come by the shop, I don't need your protection.

Jamal He ain't gonna be much different.

Angela I barely know him.

Jamal You know who I meant, then. Gonna take him to Manchester?

Angela Juss go.

Jamal Got him all lined up next, like you had me. You love it.

Angela And you love not to listen. You don't change.

Jamal   Not allowed, ennit?

Angela   See how you go?

Jamal   Ennit?

Angela   Bored now.

Jamal   Yer the only one who can change.

Angela   Believe.

Jamal (*pulls out a wad of money*)   See?

Angela   I got eyes.

Jamal   Remember when I had nuttin, niche? You paid for everything. Don't tell me I ain't changed.

Angela   You ain't changed.

Jamal   How you know?

Angela   I know.

Jamal   Thing is . . . I know you care. I saw you at the rave.

Angela   I was with my friends.

Jamal   Gimme a cuddle.

Angela *laughs.*

Jamal   Please. You want me to beg or what?

Angela   Don't beg. Tell me first.

Jamal   It's nuttin.

Angela   You only ask when you done summin bad.

Jamal   I ain't done nuttin bad.

Angela   Yet.

Jamal *looks scared.*

Angela   Come here.

Jamal *approaches* **Angela**, *who embraces him.* **Jamal** *holds her tightly.* **Angela** *pats his back like she is looking for something. She can feel a gun sticking out from his back trousers, and removes it. She pushes him away.*

Angela   Is this why you don't want me seeing him? Is he the little turd?

Jamal   No.

Angela   Who den?

Jamal   Some other guy, who I love like a brother, alright?

Angela   But you go shoot him anyway?

Jamal   I have to.

Angela   Ca yer man wants you to?

Jamal   He's telling me to.

Angela   Yer man tell you when to go take a shit? Yer a dog.

Jamal   I tell the boy not to fleece me, but he go do it anyway. I only just find out. He lied right to my face, Angela.

Angela   Leave.

Jamal   One minute my man's buying this for me, next thing he's slapping me around, calling me a ejut, telling me Ryan's selling shit behind my back, get my house in order or else. You know how that made me feel, and I don't want to feel like that. Me and my man, cruising in his four-by-four, laughing and chatting about our day, that's how I want to feel. Everything will be fine after this. I dunno, maybe you and me . . .

Angela   What shit are you bringing now?

Jamal   Angela, it don't work without you.

Angela   It don't work at all.

Jamal *takes back his gun.*

Jamal   Don't go seeing him.

Exit **Jamal**, *followed by* **Angela**.

Enter **Tash** *and* **Nathan**.

Tash   Yo?

Nathan   What?

Tash   Think yer good, then?

Nathan   At what?

Tash   Football, you think you're any good?

Nathan   I'm alright.

Tash   You must be, if Arsenal are sniffing round you.

Nathan   Then I must be good then.

Tash   You gonna take me to a game for my birthday? You gonna let me meet Thierry Henry? Are you?

Nathan   I dunno.

Tash   You an ejut?

Nathan   No.

Tash   Well, stop chatting like one.

Nathan *sighs*.

Tash   What?

Nathan   Nuttin.

Tash   Don't get fresh, boy.

Nathan   Look, what you want, Tash?

Tash   From you?

Nathan   Yes.

Tash   Nuttin.

Nathan   Can I go?

Tash   I'll come with you.

Nathan I'm going home.

Tash Yeah. I can meet your mum and dad, tell them you have a new girlfriend.

Nathan But you're not my girlfriend.

Tash Oh I see, you play for Arsenal now and you think you're all that.

Nathan No.

Tash You don't like girls? You're a batty bwoi?

Nathan No.

Tash You don't like black girls then, you a racist?

Nathan No!

Tash You want to beat me up, beat up a black girl?

Nathan Stop it, Tash.

Tash This black girl don't like racists. You want to see how much?

Tash *hits him repeatedly.*

Tash You best fight back.

Nathan No.

Tash Gonna kick yer arse.

Nathan *shoves her.*

Nathan I'm sorry.

Tash You just touch me?

Nathan Leave me alone.

Enter **Ryan**.

Tash Yer dead.

Ryan Did I see what I just saw?

Nathan I only pushed her. She was hitting me.

Ryan *slaps him.*

Ryan   Who tell you to push her?

Nathan   I want to go home.

Ryan   You know what happens to boys who beat up girls?

Nathan   Yes.

Ryan   Good.

Ryan *slaps* **Nathan** *to the floor.* **Tash** *laughs.*

Tash   Yeah, yeah, alright, Ryan. Ryan? That's enough, man, come on. Ryan? Ryan, come on, leave him alone, Ryan, enough! (*Grabs* **Nathan**.) Go home, go home.

Exit **Nathan**.

Ryan   Don't ever step in like that again.

Tash   Did someone drop you on the head when you were little?

Ryan   He was beating you up?

Tash   So?

Ryan   Next time I go leave you. Little ho.

Tash   I'm telling Kev.

Ryan   Tell him. No, don't tell him.

Tash   Yes, you go cry now.

Ryan   You get me mad. Why you love to do that?

Tash   Why you care?

Ryan   You can't be nice? Once? I can be nice.

Tash   How can you be nice? What are you going to do for me?

Ryan   Tell me what you want. I'll tek you out.

Tash   There's nowhere to go.

Ryan   Go somewhere to eat.

Tash   I ain't going McD's with you.

Ryan   Did I say McD's? I meant a proper place with knives and forks.

Tash (*laughs*)   You?

Ryan   Me.

Tash   Alright. Go on then.

Exit **Tash**.

Enter **Kev**.

The boys are playing one-on-one basketball. **Kev** *has just scored another hoop.*

Kev   Oh! And the score is now?

Ryan   Shut up.

Kev   You've no idea how much it hurts to be this good.

Ryan   Yeah, carry on.

Kev   Oh, pick up your face, man.

Ryan   Pick up yours.

Kev   Don't mek me come over there and slap you.

Ryan   If you want, try.

Kev   Right, you go tell me wass up?

Ryan   You go tell me?

Kev   Tell you what? Tell you what? Tell me before I beat you to death with this ball.

Ryan   About what you're playing at.

Kev   Play ball.

Ryan   You know what I'm chatting about.

Kev   No, I don't.

Ryan   Yes, you do.

Kev   I know you got exactly ten seconds to live.

Ryan   I saw you.

Kev   Five seconds.

Ryan   At the rave.

Kev   Two.

Ryan   Schmoozing with Jamal.

Kev   So?

Ryan   I told you what he was doing now.

Kev   So?

Ryan   And that don't bother you?

Kev   What Jamal does is up to him.

Ryan   Yeah, him going around laughing, telling everybody yer Gupta's bitch now, yeah, that's up to him.

Kev   Alright, what's going on between you two?

Ryan   What's going with you?

Kev   I asked first. Before I left, the two of you were like that. Now yer like this.

Ryan   Guy loves to laugh at me. I ask him for a little summin ever now and then, and he laughs.

Kev   But it's not every now and then, is it?

Ryan   He laughs!

Kev   You said you'll clean yourself up.

Ryan   You wouldn't laugh.

Kev   You promised me, Ryan.

Ryan   Fool thinks he's a step above now. He always did.

Kev   Are you listening to a word?

Ryan   We gotta bring him down.

Kev   He's not laughing at you. He barely sees you.

Ryan   Yeah, and on the times he sees me, he laughs. I don't want anyone laughing at us.

Kev   Whatever beef you got with Jamal –

Ryan   I'm just telling yer.

Kev   Run it by him. You get me all vex now.

Ryan   Ain't like the first time.

Kev   I can't keep doing it.

Ryan   It just makes me mad the way he goes and struts himself round here now. He thinks I'm in his pocket, it's the other way round, though. I got him so fooled. I'm doing business of my own, right here.

Kev   I don't want to hear that, Ryan.

Ryan   Jamal can do what he likes, but he ain't having this park.

Kev   Let him have it, man.

Ryan   I know you didn't just say that to me.

Kev   It's just a spot.

Ryan   This is our spot. You don't care any more. Jamal ain't tekin it. I have to say, you're letting me down big style.

Kev   Good. Now shut up.

Ryan   You shut up.

Kev   Just shut up.

Ryan   Juss don't be telling me about giving him our spot.

Kev   Is this your way of shutting up?

Ryan   Not after what we did here.

Kev (*smiles*)   I'm not telling it again.

Ryan   It's your turn.

Kev   It's yours.

Ryan   I told it last, that time in KFC, remember, when Kieron wanted to know how you and me hooked up in the first place. Dem two yats were staring from the other table, overhearing, so we checked dem.

Kev   Actually it was me and Kieron who checked dem.

Ryan   Yeah, but I checked them first, right? Right?

Kev   Yeah, I remember now. You checked them first.

Ryan   Thank you.

Kev   Then you had to go home.

Ryan   To see my brother. Yeah?

Kev   Yes. Carry on.

Ryan   It was important.

Kev   Yes.

Ryan   I thought, yeah, let Kieron have this one. His need is greater. Last time his sack was emptied was in a previous life, yeah?

Kev   Yeah!

Ryan   So carry on, it's your turn. You be Chris.

Kev   Like a baby.

Ryan   Don't say that.

Kev   Joke.

Ryan   Well?

Kev   Ere, wass yer game?

Ryan   (*mimics*)   Ere, wass yer game?

Kev   I'm playing Chris.

Ryan   Sorry.

Kev   So what you doing, pikey boy? This is our court, this is our park.

Ryan   No, it ain't.

Kev   Yes, it is. Gimme yer ball. Come on, I ain't gonna take it. I just want to see it.

Ryan *mimes giving him the ball.*

Kev   Thank you.

Ryan   Hey, gimme my ball back.

Kev   Go home, gyppo.

Ryan   Give it back, Chris.

Kev   Or what?

Ryan   Or me!

Kev   You doing me?

Ryan   Yeah.

Kev   Who's this, your brother?

Ryan   Yeah, he is, now pass the ball back, pass it back.

The boys pretend they are fighting two other boys and are winning.

Still remember like it was yesterday.

Kev   Yeah?

Ryan   Yeah what? What?

Kev   It's nuttin.

Ryan   I saw Chris the other day, hanging with his brother. All I had to do was smile at the fool and he's still running and hiding. The pair of them. He was scared, man. Like I want Jamal to be scared. You get me? Who's the bitch now?

Kev   We are.

Ryan   Whose park is it now?

Kev   It's yours.

Ryan   Who is never coming back to the park for the rest of their miserable lives?

Kev   We are.

Ryan   Believe, bitch. Now run . . .

Kev/Ryan   . . . and hide.

They laugh.

Kev   I get you.

Ryan   This is our spot.

Kev   Our spot.

Ryan   No one takes it away from us.

Kev   No one.

Exit **Kev** *and* **Ryan**.

Enter **Tash**, *followed by the Hood.*

Tash   What do you want?

Hood   See your phone.

Tash   Don't have one.

Hood   Do you want to get raped?

Tash *shows him the phone.*

Hood   What else you got?

Tash   Nuttin.

Hood   You know yer lying. (*Ogles her.*) You go show me?

Tash *unbuttons her blouse.* **Hood** *looks down.*

Hood   Nice. Do you think I'm nice?

Tash   Yes.

Hood   Say I'm nice.

Tash   Yer nice.

Hood   I look after yer phone for you. Ca I'm nice. Say thank you.

Tash   Thank you.

Hood   Tell yer brother, I'm waiting.

Exit **Hood**.

Enter **Ryan**.

Ryan   You look nice.

Tash *laughs*.

Ryan   What?

Tash   Yer dry.

Ryan   Why you running me down?

Tash   Why is yer chat dry?

Ryan   You want go?

Tash   No, let's eat. What you doing?

Ryan   Pulling out the chair for you.

Tash   Ejut.

Ryan   What you saying?

Tash   Joke.

Ryan   You want a menu?

Tash   No, let me guess what I want.

Ryan   You gotta read the menu.

Tash   So pass it.

Ryan   Why you carrying on so?

Tash   You should see me when I'm in a bad mood.

Ryan   Thought you wanted this.

Tash   I do. What is this?

Ryan   That's your choice of starters, then your main course. It's on me, yeah, have what you want.

Tash   I will.

Ryan   Nice place.

Tash   Whatever.

Ryan   My mum had her birthday party here once. That's why I remembered it.

Tash   Yeah, yeah. Don't they do burgers and fries or summin? Wass this?

Ryan   Carbonara.

Tash   And?

Ryan   It's pasta. White sauce.

Tash   Sounds renk.

Ryan   It's nice.

Tash   Get me a quarter-pounder with cheese.

Ryan   They don't do that here.

Tash   There's a McD's cross the road.

Ryan   You said.

Tash   I know what I said, now I'm saying this.

Ryan   I can't bring food in here.

Tash   Blah blah.

Ryan   We'll get fling out.

Tash   Come on, Ryan. Super size me.

Ryan   Just order summin.

Tash   I hope that ain't me you're barking at.

Ryan   I'm trying to do summin nice for you and you're taking the piss.

Tash   Summin nice! You don't know how.

Ryan   Wass up wid you?

Tash   We both know what you want.

Ryan   This is what I want.

Tash   You want me. You want grind me so bad. Are you a paedophile, Ryan?

Ryan   Move.

Tash   A nasty dirty paedophile.

Ryan   I ain't like that.

Tash   Why you always staring at me, with your tongue hanging out?

Ryan   You love to put it about.

Tash   That mek it alright?

Ryan   I ain't no perv.

Tash   But I know you want me. Do you want me, Ryan?

Ryan   Yeah.

Tash   So you are one. You and your friends who love hang round school gates, like dog –

Ryan   Tash?

Tash (*snaps*)   YOU ALL ARE! YOU ALL ARE!! Nasty . . .

Ryan   What?

Tash   Just bring me my burger, yeah.

Ryan   What is it? (*Goes to touch her.*)

Tash   Who said you could touch me?

Ryan   I was only trying to –

Tash   Go wash yourself. Wouldn't even mind so much, but you ain't even that buff. Carrying on like you all that. Fighting with Jamal. He laughs at you, everyone laughs, even Kev. You're nuttin without him.

Ryan   No.

Tash   You know it. He was rolling around on the floor when he tell me about Chris Farrant. The real story, not the rubbish you love to tell everyone. How you pissed yourself when Chris bullied you and took your ball. How you begged Kev to help you. He's always helping you. Yer Kev's bitch and you love him. Now go bring me a quarter-pounder, wid fries.

Ryan   You and your brudda.

Tash   If you're gonna start whining, I'm gone.

Exit **Tash** *and* **Ryan**.

Enter **Kev** *and* **Angela**.

Kev   Look, if he's come back, I ain't dealing with him.

Angela   Who?

Kev   That old black guy who was drunk. Tell Gupta to throw him out himself.

Angela   Actually, I was going to tell you we've got a delivery coming.

Kev   Right.

Angela   And he hasn't come back. You musta scared him off. Gupta shouldn't have done it. He only sent you cos you're the only black guy.

Kev   Nuh you think?

Angela   We keep saying the wrong thing to each other. One time Gupta asked me to deal with him.

Kev *smiles at the thought.*

Angela   Ahh, so you do know how to smile. You want go for a drink afterwards?

Kev   Not up for it.

Angela   Then be a gentleman. Walk me to the bus stop after work.

Kev   Cool.

Angela   How long were you in for?

Kev   Ten months.

Angela   You don't have to tell me what you did.

Kev   But you'd like to know. Robbery. Assault.

Angela   You?

Kev   Should see what I got away with.

Angela   Bad bwoi, Kev.

Kev   Who stacks shelves for a living. What you studying?

Angela   Journalism, politics.

Kev   Damn, girl. Can't imagine you doing that.

Angela   What can you imagine me doing? Keep it clean.

Kev   Dunno. You look like the rest of the girls round here.

Angela   Pushing buggies? Is this your world, Kev?

Kev *leans forward to give* **Angela** *a kiss. It becomes a lingering kiss, more intense.* **Kev** *slowly moves his hand up* **Angela***'s skirt,* **Angela** *feels it, pushes him away.*

Angela   Hey, you don't have to go so fast, you nuh.

Kev   I ain't.

Angela   Go slow.

Kev   I am.

Kev *tries again.* **Angela** *moves away suddenly, holding him at arm's length.*

Angela   What am I doing?

Kev   What?

Angela   Gal never listen!

Kev   Angela? What?

Angela   You know Jamal? Yes or no?

Kev   Yes.

Angela   I'm gone, yeah.

Kev   Gone? Come here, man –

Angela   What part of 'no' do you not understand?!

Kev   You love to tease. Like one a dem stupid gal who cry rape. You carry on.

Exit **Angela**.

Enter **Tash**.

Tash   I don't know!

Kev   You didn't recognise the voice?

Tash   No.

Kev   I'm waiting. That's all he said, that's it? Gonna kill him.

Tash   You don't even know who he is.

Kev   I know. Trust me, I know. (*Calls.*) So what, you gonna use my sister now?

Tash   Who you screaming at?

Kev   Is that how it go?

Tash   You go mad?

Kev   So what you tell me for? How can you tell me that and expect me to do nuttin? Telling you, trust me, yeah, that bwoi . . . he wants to die, he so wants to die.

Tash   It what he wants, you fool. He wants you to come after him.

Kev   How many times I tell you to keep away from bwois like that?

Tash   I am keeping away.

Kev   Look at how you dress. They don't care, say what you like, they tek one look . . .

Tash   So what am I supposed to do? Stay in my room until I'm fifty?

Kev   Yeah. Come.

Tash   That is so lame.

Kev   You see the way Ryan looks.

Tash   He's a perv.

Kev   You grind him?

Tash   Like I really want his ting anywhere near me.

Kev   Don't be nasty.

Tash   I'm answering the question.

Kev   You sure this guy didn't touch you?

Tash   What if he did?

Kev   You know what.

Tash   He didn't touch me.

Kev   Please don't lie, Tash.

Tash   I don't want you going back to prison.

Kev   Forget about that.

Tash   I can't forget about that.

Kev   If he touched you, I have to do summin. I have to. That's it. You're my sister, girl. No one touches you.

Tash   I can look after myself.

Kev   Hear me.

Tash   I am. You're not hearing me.

Kev   What am I supposed to do, Tash, tell me?

Tash   Nuttin.

Kev   That ain't an option.

Tash   Don't do it, please.

Kev   You must want me to. Deep down.

Tash   I ain't.

Kev   You love to big me up. I've heard you. My brother Kev gonna shoot you in the face, I was always there for you. You knew that. Well, I'm here now. So what you want? Warn off Ryan? Beat up this boy, what?

Tash *embraces him.* **Kev** *holds her in his arms.*

Tash   Tighter.

Kev *holds her tighter.*

Tash   You deaf?

Kev *holds her even more tightly.*

Kev   This is it? This is all you want your big brudda to do?

Tash (*in tears*)   Yes.

Kev   If that's how you feel.

Tash   I'm so tired.

Kev   Go to bed.

Tash (*cuddles up to* **Kev** *even more*)   No.

Kev   What you think this is? Who's my LST?

Tash   Me.

Kev   Believe.

Tash   Empty swimming pool, yeah, twenty heads jump in, swim around, twenty-four heads come back up, how is that possible?

Kev   I give up.

Tash   Mean you don't know?

Kev   Mean I'm tired.

Tash   It's still the same kids.

Kev   How?

Tash (*points to her forehead*)   Twenty foreheads.

Kev *laughs. He plants a kiss on her forehead.*

Tash   Boss still stressing you?

Kev   Guy don't even remember me. Me and Ryan were teifing from his shop when we were nine. Robbing him blind. All must look the same to him.

Tash   You gotta take it, Kev. Until you know what to do, yeah?

Kev   And where you learn to be so smart?

Tash   Can you do that?

Kev   Have to, ennit?

Tash   Don't let him take you away from me.

Kev   Bed.

Exit **Tash**.

Enter the **Hood**.

The **Hood** *finds the basketball, dribbles and shoots some hoops like* **Kev** *did in the opening scene.* **Kev** *approaches him.*

Kev (*full of quiet, simmering rage, taunting death*)   You think I'm stupid? Don't start on her. I'm gonna go back to work and make that job mine. I don't want you bothering us. So just step. I feel you every day on my shoulder, around me. You are not taking me.

Exit **Kev**.

Exit the **Hood**.

Act Two

Enter **Jamal** *and* **Ryan**.

Jamal *is pointing a gun at* **Ryan**.

Ryan Oh come on, Jamal.

Jamal Shut up.

Ryan It's me – Ryan.

Jamal Yeah?

Ryan Who loves you more than me?

Jamal You had to do it.

Ryan Do what, man?

Jamal Don't play me.

Ryan I'm not.

Jamal Is my name Kev?

Ryan What have I done?

Jamal Ask me that again, you'll see what I do.

Ryan What –

Jamal *cocks his gun.*

Ryan Joke! Joke!

Jamal Not now.

Ryan I'm sorry, dread.

Jamal That's you all over. You're sorry but you do it anyway. Don't I look after you?

Ryan Yeah, man.

Jamal So why you have to teif off me?

Ryan Nuh, man! Nuh. Nuh! Teif? From you? Nuh! Jamal?

Jamal   Yer dealing in the park. Don't lie.

Ryan   Yeah.

Jamal   Holding out on me. Where I come from, that's called teifing. You wouldn't steal from Kev, so why do it to me?

Ryan   I was gonna give the dough to you, Jamal, I swear.

Jamal   What, you get lost?

Ryan   I was just trying to play big, man, you know?

Jamal   No, I don't know.

Ryan   There's this honey I'm trying to impress. You know how it go, yeah!

Jamal   You wid a honey?

Ryan   Hard to believe, I know, but true. You can't impress some yat wid no brass in pocket, no! I weren't going to spend it all, Jamal, just enough to wet my beak a little. I wouldn't hold out on you, I swear, Jamal? Bredren!

Jamal   Don't smile at me.

Ryan   I weren't smiling. I'm not smiling.

Jamal   You don't know.

Ryan   What?

Jamal   It's not just me you're stealing from, Ryan. You trying to make me look bad?

Ryan   No! Please.

Jamal   Please don't cut it. I have to do summin, yeah, or it's me where you are. You get me?

Ryan   Well, gimme a couple of licks then, Jamal, come on, you don't need that.

Jamal   I have to.

Ryan   (*pleads*)   Jamal? Jamal!

Jamal   What you doing?

Ryan   Nuttin.

Jamal   Why you crouching yerself up like that?

Ryan (*scared*)   Dunno.

Jamal   You want go for a piss? You want go for a piss, Ryan?

Ryan (*in tears*)   I want go for a piss.

Jamal   I can't shoot you when you're standing like that. Have your piss. Well, go then, go.

Ryan *takes a leak.*

Ryan (*relieved*)   Ooooh! Nuttin like it, ennit, Jamal?

Jamal   You say so, dread.

Ryan   You want to aim that thing to the ground, Jamal, yer making me nervous.

Jamal   Don't think I can't use this.

Ryan   I know you can. Our man teach you, yeah?

Jamal   My man!

Ryan   Yes, your man.

Jamal   Yeah, he teach me. Safety off. Left hand, right hand, palms pressed together. You like that?

Ryan   Nice.

Jamal   You don't know how to play it straight, Ryan.

Ryan   I know.

Jamal   I'm running things. Kev's on the other side now, he's gone. Know yer place!

Ryan   I will from now on, I swear.

Jamal   How, Ryan? After today, you ain't doing nuttin.

Ryan   I know.

Jamal   Stop saying what you think I want to hear, stop it.

Ryan   I'm just saying I know.

Jamal   Don't get fresh.

Ryan   So why you treating yer brer like this? Who got you on the relay team at school?

Jamal   Oh, here we go again!

Ryan   Me. I spoke to Mr Nuttall, begged him on my hands and knees –

Jamal   Mr Nuttall didn't do niche and neither did you. There's summin you need to know, yeah, Ryan, Mr Nuttall was this much away from throwing yer arse off the team.

Ryan   No.

Jamal   Yes.

Ryan   No.

Jamal   Shut up. I was brought in to replace you. You only stayed cos Beau did his toes in, you remember? Ask Kev, he knew.

Ryan   Kev knew? He lied to me.

Jamal   He protected you, he always protected you. Made us protect you, I don't know why. All you ever do is take, Ryan, don't give back, not ever. Bout you brought me on to the team.

Ryan   We still won.

Jamal   Won what? Some shitty race? Some crap medal. I wouldn't get twenty pence for that. It was a joke, our whole time there was a joke. Aren't you forgetting summin?

Ryan   No.

Jamal   Zip your trouser up properly. You are so nasty.

Ryan   There's summin wrong with the zip.

Jamal   And for once in yer life, buy some soap. What you smiling at?

Ryan   I wasn't.

Jamal   Don't lie.

Ryan   Alright, I was.

Jamal   At what?

Ryan   You said buy soap.

Jamal   Ca you stink.

Ryan   You said, ask Kev. How am I gonna do that if yer gonna do shoot me?

Jamal   You still think I won't.

Ryan   No.

Jamal   You ain't nuttin but a disloyal, fool-ass, bitch-made punk.

Ryan   And yer brer.

Jamal   You shoulda left it alone.

Ryan   I know.

Jamal   No you don't. Yer ugly. Yer so bloody ugly, Ryan.

Ryan   Yeah, man, I'm ugly, too ugly.

Jamal   You'd say anything right now to get this gun outta yer face?

Ryan   Yeah. Jamal?

Jamal (*lowers the gun*)   I don't know how you do it.

Ryan (*relieved*)   Oh, bredren.

Jamal   I want my money, Ryan.

Ryan   Yeah.

Jamal   Hear me.

Ryan   I'm hearing you. What you think I'm doing?

Jamal   I don't care what you have to do, but get it for me. All of it! You understand?

Ryan   I understand you, Jamal. Thanks, yeah.

Jamal   Don't thank me. I ain't finished with you.

Ryan   Come on, Jamal, couldn't you just say you gimme licks?

Jamal   What if my man saw you? Don't run. You know, we weren't too bad as a team.

Ryan   We were one of the best.

Jamal   The best. Come here.

Ryan   No kicks, please. Don't kick me.

Exit **Jamal** *and* **Ryan**.

Enter **Angela**.

Angela   Look, I ain't no prick-teaser.

Kev *can hear every word but ignores her as he mops the floor around her.*

Angela   You said a bad bwoi is gonna mess me up. He already has. Or I should say they. Same story with me, every time. Meet a nice guy, makes me laugh with his chat. Do a little dance, mek a little love. All I need for them to do is to treat me right, all they needed to do was disrespect me every chance they get, fleece my money, go blow it on weed with their brers. If I mek up noise, I get beat. Can't find myself a nice guy.

Kev *stops mopping. He looks up at* **Angela**.

Angela   My mum says it's my fault. I can't keep away from the bad men. She's right.

Kev *approaches her.*

Angela   You know Jamal, yer like him.

Kev *takes her hand.*

Kev   No.

Kev *kisses her.* **Angela** *kisses him back. It gets passionate. Neither wants to let go of the other.*

Exit **Kev** *and* **Angela**.

Enter **Miss Jules** *and* **Tash**.

Miss Jules   Sit down. Sit down!

Tash *sits.*

Miss Jules   So?

Tash   So?

Miss Jules   I am not in the mood.

Tash   Gwan home, then.

Miss Jules   What is wrong with you?

Tash   You a doctor as well now, Miss?

Miss Jules   Fine, don't talk. The two of you, fighting over this boy again? You promised me.

Tash   You don't know nuttin, yeah.

Miss Jules   Because you never tell me.

Tash   I don't know anyone who love to chat as well as you. She called me a ho.

Miss Jules   You couldn't walk away?

Tash   Are you listening to me?

Miss Jules   Now you know what it feels like.

Tash   Your lip's still bleeding.

Miss Jules   Never mind that.

Tash Fine then, bleed all over the floor. You shouldn't have got in the way.

Miss Jules No, I should have just stood there and let you beat the hell out of each other.

Tash Donna couldn't beat me if she tried.

Miss Jules Oh, Tash.

Tash Am I as bad as Donna? Go chat to her.

Miss Jules I can't help her.

Tash She started the fight. Soon as the head finds out, she'll get excluded.

Miss Jules What do you care?

Tash I don't, that's your job. Help her.

Miss Jules Donna's been warned, she brought it on herself. She's a waste of space.

Tash You can't say that.

Miss Jules I believe I just did.

Tash Call yourself a teacher?

Miss Jules What?

Tash Do you call yourself a teacher? Step.

Miss Jules You know what, you're right. That's the last thing I am.

Tash Believe.

Miss Jules How can I be?

Tash I dunno.

Miss Jules Well, I do.

Tash What you doing?

Miss Jules Packing my things together, then I'm going to get in my car, go home and sleep for a year.

Tash   Yes, very funny, Miss.

Miss Jules   I'm glad you find it amusing, Natasha.

Tash   It was just a fight.

Miss Jules   You promised me.

Tash   It weren't a real promise. I'm always doing it. You always tell me off for it – that's what we do, Miss. Sit down, man.

Miss Jules   'Is who you barking at?'

Tash   Excuse me?

Miss Jules   'Don't tell me what to do, Miss, yeah! Dat ain't happening.'

Tash   Is that supposed to be me?

Miss Jules   'I'm going home to my bed, yu get me?'

Tash   You taking the piss outta me?

Miss Jules   Not nice, is it? I've had enough.

Tash   It was just a fight, you deaf? You said you weren't leaving. You know what, fine, bye!

Miss Jules   Good luck to you, Tash.

Tash   Shit teacher anyhow, didn't learn niche from you.

Miss Jules   What did you say?

Tash   You still here?

Miss Jules   For your information, Natasha, I'm a bloody good teacher.

Tash *grunts*.

Miss Jules   Don't do that.

Tash   I'll do what I like, you're quitting.

Miss Jules   If you opened your ears up more often –

Tash Oh yeah!

Miss Jules – you might know.

Tash Well, come then. Come on.

Miss Jules Come on what?

Tash My ears, they're well open now, teach me summin. Show me the goods – come on, Miss, impress me.

Miss Jules What is this, *Pop Idol*?

Tash You're such a good teacher.

Miss Jules Tash?

Tash Teach me summin now!

Miss Jules Lose the tone.

Tash You gonna teach me or what?

Miss Jules You are not making any sense.

Tash Teach me.

Miss Jules Natasha?

Tash Teach me.

Miss Jules Are you asking me to stay?

Tash Teach me. Teach me.

Miss Jules Don't make me slap you, yeah!

Tash Wa!

Miss Jules I shouldn't have said that.

Tash Yer bad.

Miss Jules Why can't you answer my question?

Tash (*mumbles*) I did.

Miss Jules What did you say?

Tash Forget it.

Miss Jules   Tell me what you said.

Tash   No.

Miss Jules   This is important.

Tash   For who?

Miss Jules   Can't you come out of your shell just once?

Tash   Can't you?

Miss Jules   What exactly is it that I am supposed to do? Get down?

Tash *laughs*.

Miss Jules   Hang out with you, be what you want?

Tash   Can you do that?

Miss Jules   Of course not.

Tash   So why you telling me to be what you want?

Miss Jules   I'm the teacher.

Tash   Ex.

Miss Jules   Give me a good reason to stay, then.

Tash   Find your own.

Miss Jules   Look at my face. See how tired I am. You lot with your cheek.

Tash   It's what we do.

Miss Jules   And what I do doesn't matter?

Tash   Course.

Miss Jules   So why don't you listen?

Tash   All I'm doing is messing with you. You do know that? Why can't you just chill, man?

Miss Jules   I'm sorry?

Tash   Let us have our fun, we're leaving soon anyhow, we go join the rest of the spases out there. All we want is a bit of fun, you have to take that away from us.

Miss Jules   What kind of drivel is that?

Tash   Ain't drivel, yeah, it's true. And you know it as well.

Miss Jules   You think I should stay?

Tash   Up to you.

Miss Jules   What fun exactly? Fighting? Sex up boys?

Tash   I'm not a slag!

Miss Jules   I can't be your friend and your teacher.

Tash   You're giving up.

Miss Jules   So are you.

Tash   Fine then.

Miss Jules   No Tash, it's not fine. What are we going to do about it? I'm asking you.

Tash   This is just your way of saying we have to do what you want?

Miss Jules   Is that so bad?

Tash   See?

Miss Jules   Trust me.

Tash   You don't understand.

Miss Jules   You're right, I don't understand how you kids live. How you refuse to ask yourselves hard questions about your own lives, what you want from them, your responsibilities. Respect for others, have manners, self-control. No, you're all being force-fed some retarded subculture from the good old US of A.

Tash   You turn Muslim, Miss?

Miss Jules   I am sick of losing another one of you. What is it you want from me?

Tash   You turning it down for a start, you're giving me a headache.

Miss Jules   Listen to me, I will leave.

Tash   Bye.

Miss Jules   You'll never have a teacher like me.

Tash   You love yourself up.

Miss Jules   One who cares.

Tash   Cares?

Miss Jules   Cares!

Tash   Like you care about Donna – a waste of space, you said. You can't teach her, ca you don't know what to do with her. Ca there's nuttin out there for her. Nuttin out there for me.

Miss Jules   No.

Tash   Nuttin out there for Kev, trust you . . .

Miss Jules   Tash, please.

Tash   Don't chat rubbish to me.

Miss Jules   Don't make me leave.

Tash   Stop pretending.

Enter **Zoë**.

Zoë   So how you get boys to notice you then Tash? Tash?

Tash *watches* **Miss Jules** *leave.*

Zoë   Earth calling Tash?

Tash   What, what you say?

Zoë   So how you get boys to notice you, then?

Tash   I wouldn't say anything, I wouldn't have to.

Zoë   Explain.

Tash   Well, you know, I'd juss catch deh eye. And if they're any kind of man, they'd know what to do, what to say.

Zoë   Well, what did Ryan say?

Tash   It was two summers ago, week when it was really hot?

Zoë   Yeah?

Tash   Him and Kev were playing basketball, they had their shirts off, Ryan's chest, man, fine, before he got fat.

Zoë   Yeah.

Tash   I juss kept staring at him. Next day he made his move, pulled me over on my way to school.

Zoë   What did he say?

Tash   It's what he did. You don't say nuttin, if you have to, keep it down to one word, like, 'Awright!' 'Yeah.'

Zoë   What if he asks me what my name is, I can't say awright or yeah, can I?

Tash   Awright then, say yer name if he asks yer.

Zoë   Right.

Tash   See, I ain't like you, 'My mate fancies you.' Yu gotta talk, not show. Let them do the begging, thass wat guys are for. But don't hang around, let them know, our patience wears thin.

Zoë   It's all about what others think of yer.

Tash   What else is there?

The basketball lands near the girls.

Tash (*to* **Zoë**)   Come here.

Zoë *approaches her.* **Tash** *undoes the top two buttons of* **Zoë**'*s shirt.*

Zoë   Hey!

Tash   Yer showing a lickle summin of wat you got, not getting them out. (*Has a peep.*) Big.

Zoë   Dyke!

Tash   Let's see if you learn.

The **Hood** *enters, looking for his basketball. He clicks his fingers, instructing the girls to throw him his ball.*

Zoë (*trying to act sexy*)   Awright?

Tash (*scared*)   Come, let's go.

Zoë   Who is he?

Tash   Come on.

The **Hood** *follows them. He catches up and squeezes* **Tash**'*s backside.*

Tash   Get off!

The **Hood** *does it again.* **Tash** *slaps him. The* **Hood** *slaps her back. He takes his ball and leaves.*

Zoë   Tash?

Tash   Bloody hate this!

Zoë   Yu awright?

Tash   Wat you doing, do yer top up.

Zoë   Yu said –

Tash   You said, I said! Come like Hilary.

Zoë   Who?

Tash   Hilary Lester.

Zoë   What about her?

Tash   Seventeen, man. Love to mek baby, got two a dem already, rumour she at it again.

Zoë She's pregnant?

Tash She muss love the feel of it dropping outta her legs or summin. Seventeen. Two baby fathers, nowhere in sight. Her life, done now, thass it! I don't need that.

Zoë Course.

Tash Ain't gonna happen to me.

Zoë Course not.

Tash Gonna get out of here, gonna get Kev out of here.

Zoë Course.

Tash Yeah. (*Mocks.*) Course.

Zoë Tash?

Tash Juss get outta my face, Zoë, yeah.

Zoë No.

Tash Get away from me.

Zoë I said no. I got Gareth's Gates's new song, the one you heard on the radio – you said you liked it. Wanna listen? Tash? It's up to you now. You can do whatever you want. We both can. Well, say summin. Tash? Come on, man.

Tash Jason texted me. He wants to see me later tonight. Like he thinks he can click his fingers. I don't want to see him later, Zoë, I don't.

Zoë Then don't.

Tash I won't.

Zoë Let the fool wait.

Tash Race you downstairs. One, two, three . . .

Exit **Tash**.

Zoë Hey! Love to cheat.

Tash *goes.* **Zoë** *waits. The ball lands again.* **Zoë** *picks it up. She decides to stride sexily over to the wall like* **Tash** *does, undoes her shirt buttons, and stands and waits. The* **Hood** *comes back. He clicks his fingers, indicating that he wants the ball now.* **Zoë** *holds it out, but she does not throw it. The* **Hood** *must go to her and get it, but he does not seem to mind. He takes the ball off her, eyes* **Zoë** *up and down in the process.*

Zoë *giggles to herself. It works, just like* **Tash** *had said.*

Exit **Zoë**.

Enter **Tash**, **Kev** *and* **Angela**.

Tash   Alright, do what I do.

Kev   What?

Tash   You'll see.

Kev   Tell me.

Tash (*to* **Angela**)   Is he this moany when he's with you?

Kev   Come on.

Angela   Yes, Kev, come on.

Kev   Alright!

Tash   Right, do what I do.

Kev   Which is?

Tash (*to* **Angela**)   OK?

Angela   Believe.

Kev   Yes?

Tash   Alright. Do what I do, exactly what I do. (*Counts on her hand.*) 'Bunny, bunny, bunny, bunny, whoops bunny, whoops bunny, bunny, bunny, bunny!' (*Folds her arms.*) Gwan den.

Kev   What?

Tash   Do what I just did.

Kev What, that?

Tash Yes, you fool.

Kev I ain't doing that.

Tash Come on.

Kev It's stupid.

Tash No, it ain't.

Kev No.

Tash You mean you can't.

Kev Shut up.

Tash It's alright, I understand. Ain't your fault yer soft.

Kev Soft?

Tash S-O-F-T.

Angela (*laughs*) Oh, shame.

Kev Don't believe this.

Tash Yeah yeah, come on.

Kev (*counts on fingers*) 'Bunny, bunny, bunny, bunny, whoops bunny, whoops bunny, bunny, bunny, bunny!' Happy now?

Tash You got it wrong.

Kev Shut up.

Tash I said do exactly what I do.

Kev Which I did, you blind?

Tash No, you didn't.

Kev Yes, I did.

Tash You didn't do it right.

Kev I did it exactly as you said!

Tash You didn't.

Kev (*counts on his hand*)   'Bunny, bunny, bunny, bunny, whoops bunny, whoops bunny, bunny, bunny, bunny!' That's what I did.

Tash   It's not what I did.

Kev   It is. Angela?

Tash   I'll do it again. (*Counts on her hand.*) 'Bunny, bunny, bunny, bunny, whoops bunny, whoops bunny, bunny, bunny, bunny!' (*Folds her arms.*)

Kev   That's what I did.

Tash (*giggles*)   Ain't.

Kev   I'm getting bored now.

Tash   Do it again.

Kev   'Bunny, bunny, bunny, bunny, whoops bunny, whoops bunny, bunny, bunny, bunny!'

Tash   No.

Kev   What you mean, no?

Tash   Still ain't what I did.

Kev   Yer blind.

Tash   Yer blind. (*Counts on her hand.*) 'Bunny, bunny, bunny, bunny, whoops bunny, whoops bunny, bunny, bunny, bunny!' (*Folds her arms.*)

Kev   That is what I did!

Tash   No it ain't!

Angela   Let me try.

Tash   Gwan den.

Angela (*counts on her hand*)   'Bunny, bunny, bunny, bunny, whoops bunny, whoops bunny, bunny, bunny, bunny!' (*Folds her arms.*)

Tash   She got it. See.

Kev   But that's what I did.

Tash   Nossir. (*Counts on her hand.*) 'Bunny, bunny, bunny, bunny, whoops bunny, whoops bunny, bunny, bunny, bunny!' (*Folds her arms.*)

Angela (*counts on her hand*)   'Bunny, bunny, bunny, bunny, whoops bunny, whoops bunny, bunny, bunny, bunny!' (*Folds her arms.*)

Tash   Kev?

Kev   'Bunny, bunny, bunny, bunny, whoops bunny, whoops bunny, bunny, bunny, bunny!' See?

Tash   No.

Kev   Oh man! (*To* **Angela**.) What you laughing at?

Angela   Don't bark at me.

Kev   'Bunny, bunny, bunny, bunny, whoops bunny, whoops bunny, bunny, bunny, bunny!'

Tash   No!

Kev   Yes!

Angela   Put him out of his misery, man.

Tash   No, let him figure it out for himself. If he's too stupid –

Kev   You got a slap coming.

Tash   Do it right, then. Angela, you go first. Ready, Kev? You sure now?

Kev   Hurry up.

Angela (*counts on her hand*)   'Bunny, bunny, bunny, bunny, whoops bunny, whoops bunny, bunny, bunny, bunny!' (*Folds her arms.*)

Kev   'Bunny, bunny, bunny, bunny, whoops bunny, whoops bunny, bunny, bunny, bunny!'

Tash   Still ain't getting it.

Kev   I'm gone.

Angela   Kev, just watch.

Tash   Don't help him.

Angela   But look at how sad he's getting, with those puppy-dog eyes.

Tash   Oh yeah, sweet.

Kev   Move.

Angela   Watch carefully.

Kev   Watch what?

Angela   Carefully. Tash?

Tash (*counts on her hand*)   'Bunny, bunny, bunny, bunny, whoops bunny, whoops bunny, bunny, bunny, bunny! (*Folds her arms.*)

Kev (*laughs, counts on his hand*)   'Bunny, bunny, bunny, bunny, whoops bunny, whoops bunny, bunny, bunny, bunny! (*Folds his arms.*)

Tash   Yes! Well done, bwoi.

Kev   That's all it was?

Tash   Took you long enough.

Angela   Clever boy. (*Gives him a peck on the cheek.*)

Kev   Dry.

Tash   Look how long it took you, who's the dry one?

Kev *produces a long-length red dress.*

Kev   What about this?

Tash   For what?

Kev   You like it?

Tash   I know you ain't getting that for me.

Kev   I know you best hold yer tongue, and get your arse in that dressing room and try it on.

Tash   See how long it is.

Kev   Good.

Tash   My birthday!

Kev   My money!

Tash   You don't like it, do you? Angela, tell him you hate it.

Angela   It's alright.

Tash   Lie. She too afraid to tell the truth.

Kev   Yer gonna be afraid of me in a sec.

Exit **Tash**.

Angela   Weren't that short.

Kev   Hey, don't go taking her side now, she'll eat you alive.

Angela *gives him a peck on the cheek.*

Kev   What?

Angela   For bringing me.

Kev   It's just shopping, ennit.

Angela   Now what about yer friends?

Kev   See, there you go.

Angela   What now? I want to know what they're like.

Kev   You know what they're like.

Angela   I don't.

Kev   You ever meet Jamal's friends?

Angela   Yes.

Kev   There you go, same friends.

Angela Pull that stick outta yer arse. 'Bout you bark at me.

Kev I weren't barkin.

Angela Place you under manners.

Kev You think.

Angela I know.

Kev Come.

Angela *gives him a hug and kiss.*

Kev (*holds on to her*) Where you going?

Angela See if Tash needs help.

Kev In a minute.

Kev *clasps hold of* **Angela**.

Angela *Beau garçon.*

Kev What you say?

Angela You're beautiful. So what's all this?

Kev I don't think I can do it.

Angela What, us?

Kev My life. I'm gonna slip up. I mean, why shouldn't I juss give up? Why am I getting all stressed for?

Angela If you have to ask, you know. It's alright.

Kev (*rejects her*) How can this be alright?

Angela Look at me.

Kev You should listen to your mum.

Angela Will you shut up please?

Kev I gonna come like Jamal.

Angela You ain't Jamal.

Kev   Fool still loves you.

Angela   I know that.

Kev   He's afraid to be afraid.

Angela *kisses him. She put her hand up his shirt.*

Kev   Hey! Yer hands are cold. Stop it. Angela, don't.
Come on, man.

Angela   We'll drop Tash off and go home, yeah. Do a little
dance, mek a little love.

They giggle.

Enter **Nathan** *and* **Tash**.

Nathan *is kicking his ball about. He is very skilful. He misses
a shot.*

Tash   Unlucky.

Nathan   Like you think you can do better.

Tash   Never said I could.

Nathan   Have a go. Come on, try it. See how far you get
without me getting it off yer.

Tash   Don't want to.

Nathan   Ca yer soft.

Tash   Whatever.

Nathan   Ca you know I'm better than you.

Tash   I know yer better than me.

Nathan   I know you know.

Tash   Good!

Nathan   We beat Christopher Wren last week.

Tash   Yeah?

Nathan   Four–two!

Tash   Whatever.

Nathan   No whatever about it.

Tash   Yes.

Nathan   We kicked their arses!

Tash   I'm so happy fer yer.

Nathan   Don't take the piss.

Tash   Don't make me, then.

Nathan   How?

Tash   Chatting like that.

Nathan   I'll chat how I like.

Tash   Not bothered.

Nathan   Shoulda seen me.

Tash   Yeah?

Nathan   Two–one down at half-time, we were, me on the bench.

Tash   The bench?

Nathan   Mr Cotton reckoned I'm doing too much, reckons I still need a break. A change of attitude is required, he says. Semi-finals of the cup, ain't won it in years, mega-game, Christopher Wren ain't soft, best team in the borough. I'm well up for this, so well up, and he leaves me on the bench, cos he wants to change my attitude, does that make sense to you?

Tash   Nuh, dread.

Nathan   Bloody stupid, I reckon. Well, he find out when we were two–nil down in the first five minutes. Cotton is a fool, he don't know what day it is. His tactics are all wrong, does he listen? Bring back –

Tash   – Mr Singh.

Nathan   Chris Wren are a mouthy lot as well.

Tash   Fit, though.

Nathan   Listen to me.

Tash   I am listening.

Nathan   From two–one down, we were three–two ahead by the fiftieth minute. I scored two in seventy seconds.

Tash   You?

Nathan   Me!

Tash   I wish I was there now.

Nathan   First, I fed Danny Lopez the ball, he pushed up, I followed, he then laid a pass for me to prod home.

Tash   Nice.

Nathan   Ain't finished.

Tash   Sorry.

Nathan   Before anyone knew it, I was on the ball again, fifty yards out. I glided past one defender, around another, then I guided my shot into the far corner as the last two defenders crashed into each other. Ten minutes later, I was at it again, headed the ball in with this wicked cross from Liam. Finally, last minutes of the game, Tony Sadler played a beauty ball forward, my first shot was blocked by the keeper but it bounced back off him, all for me, easy tap!

Tash   Nice.

Nathan   See?

Tash   I do see.

Nathan   I told you I knew what I was talking, told you I knew what I was doing. You got nuttin to say to me on that, Tash. You can't touch me on that.

Tash   Nathan, I know.

Nathan   You know?

Tash   Yeah.

Nathan   You don't know.

Tash   I do know.

Nathan   How do you know?

Tash   Just do.

Nathan   Don't mess around with me.

Tash   I'm not messing around with you.

Nathan   I can't take it.

Tash   I'm sorry.

Nathan   For what? That's the problem, I don't know what you're sorry for. Letting Ryan beat me up, taking the piss outta me one minute, eyeing me up the next. All year you bin doing it.

Tash   I do like you.

Nathan   Then why you do it?

Tash   Cos you're a silly little white boy. And I'm not supposed to want to be with you.

Nathan   How I know you ain't pissing about again?

Tash   I ain't.

Nathan   But how do I know that?

Tash   I dunno, I know I ain't. Have to trust me, ennit. I just want you – to want to kiss me.

Nathan   I do want to kiss you.

Tash   Without feeling scared.

Nathan   You make me scared.

Tash   I won't any more.

Nathan   Yeah!

Tash   I promise.

Nathan   Whatever, not bothered.

Tash   I've never been kissed.

Nathan   Lie!

Tash   Honestly!

Nathan   How come?

Tash   Just ain't. Grind, yeah, but kiss, nope.

Nathan *kisses her.*

Tash   If you asked me to go out, I would.

Nathan   Alright.

Tash   So?

Nathan   What?

Tash   So ask me.

Nathan   You want go out?

Tash   Yes.

Exit **Nathan** *and* **Tash**.

Enter **Ryan** *and* **Kev**.

Ryan   Its alright, man.

Kev   It's alright?

Ryan   Told yer. Jamal thinks he's bad man now. He do this to me, he can't do this to me. Cut him for me. Cut him for me, Kev.

Kev   Come on, Ryan.

Ryan   Come on what?

Kev   Leave me!

Ryan   You owe me, man.

Kev   I owe you!

Ryan   You owe me?

Kev   What I owe you? I've given you my life since I was nine, what more I owe you?

Ryan   I don't want to believe it was you that told him about the park, I don't want to believe that. So prove me wrong, cut him for me.

Kev   He found out cos yer a crackhead, ca you love to open yer mout.

Ryan   Tell me about the relay team.

Kev   What?

Ryan   You knew Nuttall wanted me out of the team, Jamal said.

Kev   Oh, Ryan.

Ryan   It's alright, it's alright, I forgive you. As long as you do this for me. Listen, yeah, Jamal's soff, he weren't man enough to kill me, I played him like a fool. Tell him I was gonna pay him back, we can take him. You and me.

Kev   I ain't cutting anyone for you.

Ryan   Oh yes, I be a good nigger, boss! I'm yer lickle bitch, boss! I aim to please, and I'm pleased to aim. You work for the coolie man. You deh bitch.

Kev   Ryan, man.

Ryan   'Ryan, man' what?

Kev   Don't do this, please.

Ryan   I know what you think of me. That I'm stupid, that I'm dumb. Well, I ain't, and I want respect, you understand? Now you Gupta's bitch, yes or no?

Kev   Move along, sir.

Ryan   You deh bitch, bwoi.

Kev   Please move along.

Ryan   I want buy summin. You don't feel shame?

Kev   Come on man, go.

Ryan   Tek yer hand off me. Coolie man's bitch. (*Yells.*) We have a coolie man's bitch working here. Yes!

Kev   You gonna go?

Ryan   Yer mama's a bitch too. I go grind her when I see her next. I go grind yer mudda. De bitch.

Kev   Yes, goodbye, sir.

Ryan   Take care of Jamal myself, don't need you.

Kev   Thank you, sir.

Ryan   You mudda go be thanking me.

Exit **Ryan**.

Exit **Kev**.

Enter **Zoë** *and* **Tash**.

Zoë   Can I open them now?

Tash   Open.

Zoë *opens her eyes. She sees* **Tash** *offering her a poster.*

Zoë   Yeah, what is it?

Tash   Have a bloody look.

Zoë *rolls it open. It is a picture of Kian from Westlife.*

Zoë   Oh, right.

Tash   Well, you love to go on about him. The amount of pictures you've got on the wall of him.

Zoë   Yeah.

Tash   Yer right, he is nice-looking in a way.

Zoë   Yeah.

Tash   Yu awready got this, ennit?

Zoë   No.

Tash   Yu don't like it then?

Zoë   No, I mean yeah. Course I like it.

Tash   Well, look happy then.

Zoë   I am happy.

Tash   I said look it.

Zoë *feigns a smile.*

Tash   Don't tek the piss, Zoë.

Zoë   Do I look like I'm tekin the piss?

Tash   Yeah.

Zoë   I like it. I love it.

Tash   Yu awright?

Zoë   Course.

Tash   Nuttin you wanna tell me?

Zoë   Like wat? Anything you want tell me?

Tash   Yeah, as it goes.

Zoë   Wat?

Tash   Nathan. Took me out last night.

Zoë   Is it?

Tash   Yep.

Zoë   So, where you go?

Tash   Pizza first. Cinema.

Zoë   Yawn!

Tash   Shut up, it was nice.

Zoë Dry.

Tash Why? Why is it dry? Ca he don't want to get under my skirt first?

Zoë Awright, ease up.

Tash It was nice.

Zoë Like Nathan would know what to do?

Tash He kisses better than Jason.

Zoë No.

Tash How would you know?

Zoë I don't. I juss don't believe that someone like Nathan could ever kiss better than Jason.

Tash Don't believe everything the guys round here say, when it comes down to it, they're juss boys.

Zoë Whatever.

Tash Don't patronise me, Zoë.

Zoë I ain't patronising you.

Tash 'Bout whatever.

Zoë Rah, man.

Tash What did you say?

Zoë Nuttin. So how was it? What did he do?

Tash Nuttin. At first! He was so shy.

Zoë (*disgusted*) Oh, man!

Tash I thought he was sweet.

Zoë Since when you go fer sweet?

Tash Well, you've changed.

Zoë Believe.

Tash Besides, did I say I was going for him?

Zoë   Yes.

Tash   No, I bloody didn't.

Zoë   Yeah.

Tash   I'm jokin wid you.

Zoë   Cool.

Tash   I am.

Zoë   Whatever, man.

Tash   Say again?

Zoë   Whatever. Do want you want wid Nathan.

Tash   I don't want to do nuttin wid Nathan.

Zoë   Cool den.

Tash   Don't tell nobody.

Zoë   (*laughs*)   That you don't want nuttin to do wid Nathan?

Tash   Better not.

Zoë   I won't.

Tash   Let's go out later.

Zoë   Can't.

Tash   Why?

Zoë   Gotta stay in. Mum said.

Tash   Tomorrow.

Zoë   Maybe.

Tash   You bin well busy lately.

Zoë   No.

Tash   You have. You got man or what?

Zoë   No.

Tash   You love to lie.

Zoë Am I lying?

Tash Yeah you are.

Zoë No, Tash.

Tash I saw you.

Zoë Saw me where? What?

Tash You and Jason. You and him, going to that rave at Sinclair House.

Zoë What, you doing spying on me?

Tash Ca yer a lying bitch.

Zoë Why you getting stressed?

Tash Yu tink you a proper sista now, Zoë?

Zoë Wass yer problem, yer going out wid Nathan now.

Tash I don't care about Nathan. I don't care about Jason.

Zoë So what is it then?

Tash I saw you. I didn't want to believe it, I still don't.

Zoë Wass yer problem?

Tash He grind you yet? He grind yer?

Zoë Girl mad.

Tash Did he?

Zoë Yes.

Tash He like it when you go on top, Zoë?

Zoë (*with relish*) Yes!

Tash Yu ride him!

Zoë Nuff times.

Tash Thass what he's gonna say to his bredrens, gal ride wid me, all round here.

Zoë   I'm juss having a laugh.

Tash   Stupid cow.

Zoë   Move!

Tash   You cussing me now, Zoë, you tink yer so bad?

Zoë   You said for me to do this, you said it! Now yer bitching.

Tash   It's all an act!

Zoë   Jason's juss a laugh.

Tash   Thought you were better than that. What you had was better.

Zoë   You think I was happy wid the way I was?

Tash   You were you!

Zoë   Getting picked on by you lot.

Tash   I bloody wanted to –

Zoë   What, you wanted to be like me? (*Roars with laughter.*) Tough gal Tash wanted to be like me!

Tash   Yu saw through me.

Zoë   Wait till I tell everyone.

Tash   Yu tell anyone that, and you die.

Zoë   I'll tell who I want.

Tash   Yu want to act like a ho now, Zoë? Yu want man to love you up bad? Well, yer gonna learn, bitch. Yu cuss me one time, yeah, you look at me in any way I don't like, I will cut you. I will cut you.

Zoë   How you know I won't cut you?

Enter **Kev** *and* **Jamal**.

Jamal   There's this girl I was seein. She was nice. Had a brain man, so big, smart, knows shit. Anyhow, I knew she

weren't the type that would let you rush it, but you know,
the more she won't, the more you want to. I took her out
one night, to this banging restaurant, make her feel sweet,
me as well. I was nervous. Gal made me nervous, I shoulda
known summin was up with even then. Anyhow, we're inside
yeah, and there's this mile-long queue of people in front, all
getting vex cos the restaurant has somehow messed up their
group bookings. There was this young waitress girl at the
front dealing with it all, dizzy sort, making things worse.
Couldn't speak much English either. I was well up for hitting
somebody and it was gonna be this waitress. First time ever,
I made an effort to take a girl out, and she's screwing it up.
Anyhow, this girl, my date, it's like she could read minds,
Kev, she strokes the side of my face, like she's saying,
'Nuttin's gonna spoil tonight, nuttin can, calm yerself down.'
And I did. Like her words put me in a trance. Next thing
I know, she makes her way to the front of the people, starts
helping this girl sort the orders out, speaking in French to
her. Then she's laughing and chatting with the rest of the
other people, calming them down, all I could was watch
her, Kev. Thinking to myself, how did she do that, how . . .
I couldn't, if it was juss me deh, I'd be cussing and fighting
my way out of there by then. Not her. Not many black
chicks I know could do that, you nuh, Kev, only the ones
who got summin going on inside there. She had it, whatever
it is. A gift. I knew, right there and then how loved up I was.
When things got mad, and they always do, I could always go
to her, escape fer a bit. Cuddle up. You know, feel normal.

Kev   I didn't know she was your woman.

Jamal   You'll find out, Angela ain't nobody's woman. But
there were some things she wanted I just couldn't give, you
understand? So according to her, I don't have much of a say
in who steps to her from now on, if any, right? I know that.
But I need to ask you summin, yeah, and I need you to ask
me honestly. You like her?

Kev   Well, she's fine, you know that.

Jamal   Do you like her, Kev?

Kev   It's more than that.

Jamal   Cool. That's cool. But there's one thing that's cloudy, yeah, and I need yer help in clearing it up. If your intentions are serious, i.e. you turn civilian now, want to earn a nice weekly minimum wage, that's fine, and if Angela wants to follow you, that's fine too, I got what I want and more, Angela didn't want anything to do with that, so she wave bye-bye, that's cool, I have to live with that, deal with what I got. And if anyone try grab what I got, I cut them, yeah?

Kev   Yeah.

Jamal   And if anyone is making promises to Angela, when deep down they know it's nuttin but bullshit, then come reach for me.

Kev   What?

Jamal   I'm gonna cut dem too.

Kev   Hold up –

Jamal   Understand me?

Kev   Is who you threatening?

Jamal   You, Kev. I ain't the same boy I was when you left.

Kev   None of us are.

Jamal   Believe.

Kev   What you going on with?

Jamal   You see Ryan's face?

Kev   I see it.

Jamal   You have an opinion on that? Little bastard's been holding out on me, Kev.

Kev   I said it has nuttin to do with me.

Jamal I told you.

Kev You deaf?

Jamal You told me he wouldn't.

Kev He's stupid.

Jamal I can't have that.

Kev (*laughs*) So what you gonna do? Beat up on him some more?

Jamal (*with anger*) I don't think you listening, dread.

Kev (*realises*) Oh, come on. This is Ryan, man.

Jamal A teif! And I have to deal with him for good now, I'm getting pressure from above.

Kev It's Ryan, Jamal.

Jamal I know! Relay team, brers together, for ever and ever, I know. I gave him time, he's run out. Ain't my fault. It ain't my fault. So, what you gonna do? I need to know what you're gonna do.

Kev Nuttin.

Jamal Good. Keep stacking your shelves, don't worry yerself.

Kev You know he can't pay.

Jamal It's him or me. Don't look at me like that. If you were me a year ago, Ryan would be dead.

Kev Well, lucky Ryan.

Jamal Lucky Angela.

Kev You know what, forget it. Go play hard man if you must.

Jamal I ain't playing.

Kev You want the fool, go get him. Bin looking after him since I was nine, glad to get rid of him.

Jamal   As long as we both know.

Kev   Beg you, just leave me.

Jamal   That's it, that's it. That's where I want you from now on, begging me to leave you. That's nice, that's beautiful. Ca I want to be seeing you coming a mile away, I'm the top-shotter now! So don't plan on making a comeback, Mr Shelf-Stacker. You like that? Mr Shelf-Stacker. Bad bwoi Kev, him fall from grace. What happened in Feltham, what did they do to you? Don't go warning Ryan now, Shelf-Stacker. You look after Angela. You mind yerself with her.

Exit **Jamal**.

Enter **Miss Jules**.

Miss Jules   So, are you going to tell me?

Tash   Tell you what?

Miss Jules   You don't have to feel ashamed.

Tash   I don't know what dis woman's chattin bout?

Miss Jules   Dis woman? Dis woman! You mean thiss woman standing right here . . .

Tash   Why you love to mek up noise?

Miss Jules   Bout dis woman! I'm curious. I want to know who he is.

Tash   He was juss a boy, he ain't nuttin. Besides, I chucked him.

Miss Jules   So you were stuck on him.

Tash   I chucked him.

Miss Jules   That's not what I asked.

Tash   Can we move on, please?

Miss Jules   Well, at least tell me the boy's name.

Tash   Why?

Miss Jules   I'm nosy.

Tash   Nathan.

Miss Jules   Nathan!

Tash   Yes, Nathan. Gwan laugh, then.

Miss Jules   I'm not laughing. Do you like him?

Tash   Yes, I like him.

Miss Jules   You haven't chucked him.

Tash   No.

Miss Jules (*smiles*)   Well, crack a smile, girl.

Tash   Don't tell no one, yeah?

Miss Jules   Who am I gonna tell?

Tash   Dem round here will juss laugh.

Miss Jules   Why would they laugh?

Tash   Cos I'm going out wid sum silly little white boy.

Miss Jules   Can't be that silly if you are seeing him.

Tash   But it's what they think.

Miss Jules   Never mind what they think. As long as he makes you happy. Feel special.

Tash   He does. He does all that. He's a bit soff at times, but I'll toughen him out.

Miss Jules   Not too much. Don't turn him into something he isn't.

Tash   I never thought I'd go out wid someone like him, man.

Miss Jules   Don't make yer life go cheap.

Tash   Whatever.

Miss Jules   I mean it.

Tash   I know.

Miss Jules   Where's he taking you for your birthday?

Tash   Rave.

Miss Jules   Are you sure you're not taking him?

Tash   Believe. I don't blame you. For going.

Miss Jules   You keep being this nice to me, I might just –

Tash   – stay?

Miss Jules   I can't do that. Be alright, Tash.

Tash *leaves the classroom. She approaches* **Kev**.

Tash (*teasing*)   'Bunny, bunny, bunny, bunny . . .'

Kev   Shut up.

Tash   What noise annoys a noisy oyster?

Kev   A noisy noise annoys a noisy oyster!

Tash   Whoa! Kev get a brain.

Kev   Or maybe you ain't as smart as you think.

Tash   Na! Not possible.

Kev   Be good.

Tash *gives him a peck on the cheek.*

Enter **Nathan**, *followed by* **Ryan**.

Ryan   Hey, Tash! Tash!

Tash   It's alright.

Nathan   If he starts, I'm going.

Ryan   Where you going?

Tash   Inside.

Ryan   No, you're not.

Tash   Don't touch me.

Ryan   I'm just saying.

Tash   I don't want you touching me.

Ryan   Don't go in there.

Tash   Bye.

Ryan   Don't diss me, Tash.

Tash   I'll do what I like.

Ryan   Trying to help you.

Tash   You stink.

Ryan   Jamal is in there.

Tash   I don't care.

Ryan   Listen to me.

Tash   No.

Ryan   Jamal's in there –

Tash   Nigger deaf.

Ryan   I'm gonna –

Tash   Don't care, I don't care.

Ryan   I'm telling you for the last time, don't go in there.

Tash   And I'm telling you, go wash yerself.

Exit **Tash** *and* **Nathan**.

Ryan *takes out his gun. He follows* **Tash** *and* **Nathan** *into the rave. Sound of shooting and people screaming.*

Miss Jules *bursts into tears before leaving.*

Enter **Angela**.

Angela   Who was the boy?

Kev   Some white boy, I dunno.

Angela   How's yer mum?

Kev   Won't stop crying. Driving me mad.

Angela   Talk to me. Kev?

Kev   Did you love him? Jamal?

Angela   No.

Kev   You saying you never loved him?

Angela   He would never let me. Kev?

Kev   In Feltham, yeah, it don't tek long to know how bad you are. I knew from my first day, first night, dat I weren't bad. None a dat. All dem boys deh, dat place is killing dem. Mekin dem not care. I could see it doing it to me. Mekin me think I'm badder dan I was. One guy I was in deh wid, Joel, bawled all night on his first night in. Wouldn't shut up. Next night he hung himself. No one that young should die like dat. I don't wanna die.

Angela   Come to Manchester with me.

Kev   You mad?

Angela   Come wid me.

Kev   You shouldn't say that.

Angela   Why shouldn't I say that if I mean it.

Kev   You want me to come up north wid you?

Angela   Yes!

Kev   Gal, you barely know me.

Angela   Please don't call me that.

Kev   But you don't.

Angela   I know enough.

Kev   And what you don't know you'll find in Manchester. By den it'll be too late. Yer stuck wid me. You'll be disappointed, you want get rid of me.

Angela No.

Kev Juss forget it, yeah, ain't gonna happen.

Angela Why?

Kev Forget it.

Angela Why? Tell me why? What you fraid of?

Kev Who says I'm fraid?

Angela Yer eyes do.

Kev I juss don't want you getting all stressed up deh. Yu don't want dat.

Angela All I want is for you to come wid me. We'll deal with the rest later.

Kev Didn't you hear what I said, what I'm telling you? Look at what's happened, Angela – Tash, Jamal . . . this is it, where I come from.

Angela I know where you come from.

Kev You don't know.

Angela Why you doing this?

Kev You juss love yer bad men too much, no matter what. Dis juss a game to you.

Angela No, it's not.

Kev Don't play wid me, Angela.

Angela It's not. Yer wrong.

Kev Yu love yer bad men! Yu love dem, Angela. And you gonna keep on lovin dem till you find sum nice boring white guy to marry, believe.

Angela What are you going on wid? Where you going? Yer not going, you don't chat shit to me, and juss go.

Kev Move, Angela.

Angela Talk to me.

Kev Move.

Angela This is stupid.

Kev Yeah, dass me, stupid. My life is stupid. You don't want dat.

Angela I want you.

Kev Yu want hear how I get beat up every night, by my cellmate? Yu want hear how I have to fight with myself, every day?

Angela I'm not blind.

Kev Part of me, yeah, part of me juss wants to run out wid my brers, find the rass who shoot up my sister, do some shit. Any kind of shit! Anything, dass better dan stacking shelves fer de the rest of my life. I'm gonna do it, Angela.

Angela No.

Kev I was top shotter. I could earn more in a day than Gupta gives me in a week.

Angela Don't say that.

Kev Why shouldn't I do it?

Angela Yes, Kev, why?

Kev Don't you get it, man?

Angela Don't you get it? I know you're afraid, But hear what, I'm afraid too. I'm afraid that you're going to let me down like every other man in my life. But I can't help how I feel, yeah. I can't help how I feel about you.

Kev I can't hold out. But I can't go back.

Angela Let me help you.

Kev Should listen to yer mum, Angela.

Angela Kev.

Kev   Gal don't listen.

Angela (*holds him*)   Let me.

Exit **Angela**.

Enter **Ryan**.

Ryan   Go? Go where?

Kev   Up north, Manchester, with Angela. I can't stay here.

Ryan   Bredren!

Kev   What did you say?

Ryan   Huh?

Kev   Bredren?

Ryan   You are.

Kev   My sister's dead.

Ryan   Yeah. I know.

Kev   You know? Say it.

Ryan   Say what?

Kev   Say 'My sister's dead. Tash is dead.'

Ryan   Kev, man.

Kev   Say 'Tash is dead.' Say 'Jamal is dead.' Your friend, our friend, my sister. They're both dead!

Ryan   What you want . . . ?

Kev   Say it!

Ryan   Tash is dead, Jamal is dead.

Kev   I'm so scared.

Ryan   Don't say that.

Kev   I'll say what I like – you've never been scared? You only pretended to be scared, pissing yourself when the Farrant brothers were picking on you, is that it?

Ryan   You shouldn't have told her that.

Kev   I didn't know she was going to open her mouth.

Ryan   She love to laugh at me.

Kev   You were always looking at her. Why couldn't you leave her alone?

Ryan   She was putting it about nuff times.

Kev   Don't.

Ryan   Ask any brer round here.

Kev   You want die?

Ryan   Carrying on, acting all sweet in that red dress, what she expect guys to do?/

Kev   / I don't want to hear.

Ryan   / hold it in?

Kev   Red dress?

Ryan   Yeah.

Kev   How you know she was wearing it?

Ryan   I see her in it.

Kev   When?

Ryan   What you want?

Kev   When?

Ryan   Nuff times.

Kev   Nuff times?

Ryan   Wass up with you?

Kev   You saw her wearing it nuff times?

Ryan   Yes.

Kev   Yer lying.

Ryan   What you chatting about?

Kev   You say you saw her wear it nuff times.

Ryan   Yeah!

Kev   Yer lying!

Ryan   How am I lying?

Kev   She only bought it the other day. I got it for her as a birthday present. Last night was the first night she wore it.

Ryan   Yeah?

Kev   How did you know she wearing it?

Ryan   It was her other red dress.

Kev   No, she ain't got another red dress. She only had that one! How did you know she was wearing it?

Ryan   Saw her.

Kev   Where? Where did you see her?

Ryan   Around.

Kev   Did you see her around at the rave? Ryan, did you see her at the rave?

Ryan   Maybe I did.

Kev   What kind of an answer is that?

Ryan   Look, if you want to go off with your yat, it's cool.

Kev   Is it?

Ryan   Turn soff from time.

Kev   Did you kill my sister, Ryan, you shoot her?

Ryan   Can't believe yer asking this.

Kev   Did you shoot my sister, Ryan? You shoot my sister? You shoot my sister?

Ryan   Stop asking me that.

Kev   You shoot my sister?

Ryan   Stop asking me.

Kev   You shoot my sister?

Ryan   Stop it.

Kev   You shoot my sister?

Ryan   Stop asking me.

Kev   You shoot my –

Ryan   I tell her don't laugh at me. Too many times I let her get away with it. No more. Weren't even her I was reaching for, it was him. I knew he was going to that rave, I wanted to put a bullet in his face, I wanted him to come out, I see him, see her, with that little fool of a white boy, all the time she liked him, she got me to beat him up one time, she was playing me. Why you have to tell her about the Farrants? That was our secret, boss. Ours. No one else needed to know. Did you really think Tash could keep a secret? I told you to take care of Jamal. Going on about you want to change, how long you really think you woulda last in Gupta's? Tell the truth, confess? Ejut.

Kev   You shoot my sister.

Ryan   Didn't mean to, maybe I did. Dunno. Maybe Jamal was the one, I was aiming at him. But she was an accident, she got in the way. Maybe. Maybe she saw me there. She lips up her stupid white boy in front of me, on purpose like, maybe that was it. I didn't care no more. Left hand right, all that. Maybe. All I wanted was our spot.

Kev   Fuck the spot.

Ryan   Fuck us as well, ennit, Kev. It's all I got. You're all I got. It don't work without you.

Kev   It's you. Isn't it? He couldn't get me by himself.

Ryan   Who is he?

Kev   He sent you.

Ryan   Who?

Kev   You lickle pussy bastard you! Come, come get me.

Ryan   Kev?

Kev (*jabbing at* **Ryan**)   Come get me. You got my sister,
now come get me. I'm a bad bwoi, right! From time.
'Summin you want, my friend, a little pop, keep you on top,
couple of rocks, what you need?' Can't work in supermarket,
can't love no woman, all I can do is this, so tek me, tek me
now, come on, big man!

Ryan   Kev!

Kev   Yer soff! The big D! Yer soff, gw'y!

Kev *breaks down.* **Ryan** *holds him.*

Ryan   It's like it weren't me doing it.

Kev   Who then?

Ryan   I'm so tired.

Kev   So go sleep.

Ryan   Then what?

Kev   I'll think of summin.

Ryan   Yer my brer.

Kev   For ever.

Kev *gently holds his arm around* **Ryan***'s neck. He squeezes.* **Ryan**
cannot breathe. He whispers to **Kev** *for him to stop, but* **Kev** *tightens
his grip until* **Ryan** *passes out.* **Kev** *gently lays* **Ryan***'s lifeless body
on the ground.*

Enter the **Hood**. *He throws* **Kev** *the basketball.*

Blackout.